DATE DUE

OC ~~__ '__~~	NO 28-05		
MR 12 '93	DE 17 '05		
OC 15 '93	DE 21 '07		
OC 29 '93			
DE 3 '93			
MR 18 '94			
MY 13 '94			
AG 18 '94			
DE 2 '94			
JY 13 '95			
JY 25 '96			
AP 28 '97			
AG 8 '97			
DE 17 '97			
JA 28 '__			
DE __ __			

DEMCO 38-296

THE ONE HOUR
COLLEGE APPLICANT

REVISED EDITION

The One Hour
COLLEGE APPLICANT

You don't need to read
a 300-page book to apply to college!

Lois Rochester & Judy Mandell

Graphics by James A. Sullivan
Book design by Clair Stamatien

Mustang Publishing Co.
Memphis, TN

Copyright © 1989, 1990 by Lois Rochester and Judy Mandell.

Distributed to the trade by National Book Network, Inc.

This book is available at special discounts for quantity purchases by schools, libraries, and other businesses. For information, please contact Mustang Publishing.

Library of Congress Cataloging-in-Publication Data

Rochester, Lois, 1928 -
    The one hour college applicant : you don't need to read a 300-page book to apply to college / Lois Rochester & Judy Mandell ; graphics by James A. Sullivan.
      p.   cm.
    Includes bibliographical references (p.).
    ISBN 0-914457-38-1 (alk. paper)
    1. College applications -- United States -- Handbooks, manuals, etc.
2. Universities and colleges -- United States -- Admission -- Handbooks, manuals, etc.   I. Mandell, Judy, 1939 -   . II. Title.   III. Title: 1 hour college applicant.
LB2351.52.U6R63   1990
378.1' 056 -- dc20   90-42471
                                              CIP

Printed on acid-free paper. ∞

10 9 8 7 6 5 4 3 2 1

ACKNOWLEDGMENTS

*T*hanks to the following who gave of their time (just an hour, of course) to read our manuscript: Sarah Beaumont, Meryl Bertenthal, Alexandra Daniel, Margery Daniel, Marie Derdeyn, Esther Freix, Jessica Andrus Lindstrom, Gerald Mandell, Noora Niskanen, Raili Niskanen, and Roberta Platts-Mills.

Lois Rochester
Judy Mandell

5

CONTENTS

Why "The *One Hour* College Applicant"?

We've counseled hundreds of students on how to choose a college and survive the college application process. Over the years, we grew increasingly dismayed at the guidebooks available to help them through the experience. Some of the books seemed to get so big and dense that all their valuable advice was lost in a sea of words. Other books became so specialized that it took a whole stack of them to cover the admissions process from beginning to end.

It got to the point that it took three days to read all you needed to know to fill out a four-page college application! Instead of making the admissions process easier, these books were actually making students more frightened and anxious about college and their applications.

So we decided to write a book that would contain the vital advice and information students need, but in an easy-to-read format. We thought students would welcome a short, inexpensive guide with all the basic admissions information – as long as it didn't take forever to find the details they needed. And, if they required more help on a specific topic (like the essay or financial aid), we decided to list dozens of books, organizations, hotlines, and other resources for assistance. These are resources we've used over the years, and we know they are valuable and worthwhile.

So if you're looking for creaky stories about what college admissions was like in the 1930's or heart-warming anecdotes about "the kid with dyslexia who wrote a simple but beautiful essay and got into Harvard," you've got the wrong book. But if you're looking for a no-nonsense, nuts-and-bolts guide to the entire college admissions process, *The One Hour College Applicant* is for you.

The Importance of College

Now don't get us wrong. Just because our book has fewer than 300 pages doesn't mean we are cavalier (there's a good SAT word!) about college or your application. Choosing a college is a major life decision. It will affect your career choice, your income, where you live, your friends, and perhaps your mate.

And working on the application to the college of your choice is just that – *work*. It's not a simple matter of fill-in-the-blanks. If you're applying to a selective school, the competition for admissions can be brutal and the application will require serious effort, so don't blow it.

However, applying to college is not brain surgery, so don't get ulcers about it. Yes, the admissions process can be time-consuming, complicated, and frustrating. But it is manageable if you work through it step-by-step. (After all, about 1.2 million high school students somehow manage it each year.)

About This Book

Although this book is primarily for high school students, most of the information will also be useful to adults starting or returning to college. Further, we hope parents of college applicants will find it helpful in understanding just what their kids are going through.

The book is roughly divided into four segments. Chapters 1-4 give general information about colleges and admissions requirements. Chapters 5-10 help you through the admissions process from beginning to end. Chapter 11, "What If?", addresses a number of special situations that might occur. Chapter 12 lists a variety of resources for additional information on all the topics covered in the book.

Please note that all data (grades, costs, etc.) are derived only from our knowledge and experience, not from statistical studies or surveys. We present data as general guidelines, not as indisputable facts.

By the way, we welcome your comments and suggestions. Please write to us in care of the publisher.

Bon Voyage!

You are about to begin some of the best, most exciting years of your life. College will give you an opportunity to meet a wonderful diversity of people and to explore ideas, subjects, and interests that you may never get a chance to investigate again. We encourage you to take full advantage of these special years, and we hope your entire college experience – from the first list you write of possible college choices to the time you receive your diploma – is wonderful and enriching.

Good luck!

Chapter I:

Thinking about College

Thinking about College

Things to consider before you start your college admissions process:

- There are many reasons for going to college — preparing for a job or career; gaining new knowledge and skills; having fun. Your first job is to **clarify your own goals** so you can aim your college search appropriately.

- There's a wide range of college choices — about 3,400 schools in the U.S., ranging from highly selective to non-competitive. Almost anyone who wants a college education can get one.

- The responsibility for choosing colleges and applying is **yours**, not your parents' or your guidance counselors'.

 There isn't just one best college for you. More likely, there are several. And there may be some wrong schools. You may have to make compromises.

- Pinpoint the range of colleges that meet your needs, where you'll have a chance for admission. Try not to overestimate or underestimate yourself. Be realistic.

- Aim for the best college possible, but remember that prestige does not necessarily mean "best" for you. You might be miserable in a "name" college but thrive in one that is less well-known.

- Your parent's college or the colleges that are "in" with your friends might not be the best for you either. Dare to be different.

- In the beginning stages of the application process, don't rule out any college on the basis of cost, location, or anything else. Be open-minded. You'll change your mind as you go along.

- College is primarily an academic experience. If you have never been a good student and dislike studying, but you enjoy hands-on activities, think about a technical school or at least a career-oriented college. Consider getting non-traditional college credits.

☛ For more information: *Bear's Guide to Earning Non-Traditional College Degrees.*

> ***Y**ou don't have to have a college degree to succeed in life. And you don't have to go to college right after high school. Adult education and training will be available throughout your life.*

❑ You may want to attend college part-time and take longer than four years to graduate.

❑ College pays in the long run. Those with college degrees earn more on average than those without degrees.

❑ Getting in a college doesn't guarantee success and/or happiness. It's what you do there that counts.

❑ Throughout the process, talk with your guidance counselor, teachers, parent(s), family members, and friends to sound out your ideas and get theirs.

❑ The thought of going to college, away from home and friends, can be scary. Try not to let this keep you from going ahead with your plans.

❑ The thought of making decisions about where to apply and where you'll go is also scary, but it's not the end of the world if you make wrong ones. You can transfer, if necessary.

❑ Public school students have just as good a chance of getting into the most selective colleges as do private school students.

You can ask someone (parent or friend) to help you do some of the work of applying to colleges:

- getting school transcripts
- planning and arranging visits
- sending for information
- screening guidebooks to develop an initial list
- typing, copying, and mailing final application forms
- talking to guidance counselors, family members, and friends to get ideas and information
- reading resource books, such as those on financial aid

❑   Be wary if you're asked to send money to have your name on an impressive sounding list of successful high school students. Ask your guidance counselor. Such a listing probably **won't** help your chances of admission.

❑   The process of applying to college is a learning experience. You'll learn about yourself, your family, and financial realities. You'll meet new people and possibly travel to new places. Whatever the final outcome, it can be time and effort well spent. Enjoy it!

❑   If you think you may not go to college right after high school, take the college tests and get recommendations from teachers anyway. Your application folder will then be in order if you change your mind later.

Chapter II:

Overview of Colleges:
Types • Programs • Size • Selectivity • Costs • Consortia

Overview of Colleges:

Types • Programs • Size • Selectivity • Costs • Consortia

There are many different types of colleges: public, private, two-year, four-year, liberal arts, technical, single-sex, co-ed, and so on. They vary in programs and degrees offered, size, selectivity, costs, and numerous other ways.

Types of Colleges

TWO-YEAR COLLEGES: community, junior, or technical

❑ often less selective and less expensive than four-year colleges

❑ primarily occupational or pre-professional; some also offer liberal arts

❑ award certificates or associate degrees (A. A. or A. S.)

❑ some have transfer programs to four year colleges

❑ housing available at some junior colleges but usually unavailable at community and technical colleges

FOUR-YEAR COLLEGES

❑ award undergraduate bachelor degrees (B.A. or B.S.)

❑ some also award associate degrees

UNIVERSITIES

❑ undergraduate four-year colleges plus graduate schools

❑ undergraduate colleges predominate at some; graduate schools predominate at others

❑ undergraduates may have opportunities for graduate study and research

PUBLIC COLLEGES AND UNIVERSITIES

In general:

- many have strict grade point average (GPA) and standardized test score cut-offs for admission

- some have open admissions for state or city residents

- may have limited housing for students

In-state:

- relatively low cost

- admissions preference usually given to in-state applicants

Out-of-state:

- higher tuition than for in-state applicants

- often higher admissions standards than for in-state applicants

- more limited chances for admission. Although some state colleges admit more than 50% of out-of-state applicants, 10% to 20% is more usual, and some admit only 2% to 4%.

PRIVATE COLLEGES AND UNIVERSITIES

- generally cost more than in-state public colleges

- less likely to have standardized test score and GPA cut-offs than public colleges

- tend to look at the total applicant, not just objective data

MILITARY ACADEMIES AND COLLEGES

U. S. Military Academies: Air Force, Army, Coast Guard, Merchant Marine, Navy

- ❏ co-ed

- ❏ highly selective for admission

- ❏ tuition free, but post-graduation military service required

- ❏ offer mostly science and technology majors; some liberal arts

- ❏ require rigorous physical training and discipline

Other Military Colleges

- ❏ about ten public or private two- and four-year colleges

- ❏ Reserve Officer Training Corps (ROTC) programs

- ❏ military service may or may not be required

    ☞ For a list of public and private colleges with Army ROTC programs, including military colleges, see *Peterson's Guide to Four Year Colleges.* For more information: Air Force ROTC; Army ROTC; Navy-Marine Corps ROTC.

SINGLE-SEX COLLEGES

- ❏ very few all-male, but more than 90 all-female two- and four-year colleges

- ❏ somewhat less competitive admissions at the most selective women's colleges than at comparable co-ed colleges

> **Graduates of women's colleges are more likely to enter traditiona male fields.**

- ❏ may offer more academic encouragement, leadership, and extra-curricular opportunities for women

- ❏ graduates of women's colleges more likely to go to graduate school, enter traditional male fields, and earn higher salaries than female graduates of co-ed colleges

  ☛ For more information: *Women's College Coalition*

RELIGIOUS-ORIENTED COLLEGES / BIBLE COLLEGES

- ❏ high percentage of students and faculty belong to particular religious faiths

- ❏ emphasis on such courses as religion, theology, and Bible studies

- ❏ may have strict student behavior rules

  ☛ For more information: *Bear's Guide to Earning Non-Traditional Degrees;* American Association of Bible Colleges

BLACK COLLEGES

- ❏ approximately 100 predominantly black colleges exist, mostly in the South

- ❏ may offer black students better opportunities for personal and academic growth than predominantly white colleges

- ❏ costs may be lower and admissions criteria somewhat more lenient than at comparable predominantly white colleges

  ☛ For more information: *The Black Student's Guide to Colleges; I Am Somebody*

LIBERAL ARTS

❑ traditional courses and majors in subjects such as English, history, psychology, biology, language, fine arts

❑ broad-based preparation for work or graduate school

OCCUPATIONAL OR PRE-PROFESSIONAL

❑ usually some liberal arts courses required

❑ variety of career-oriented majors such as business administration, medical technology, elementary teaching

COMPREHENSIVE

❑ liberal arts and occupational or pre-professional courses and majors

SPECIALIZED OR SINGLE-PURPOSE

❑ for those certain about career choices, such as music, art, aeronautics, business, engineering, Bible studies

SPECIAL

❑ Cooperative (CO-OP) Education

• courses and paid jobs, alternating or in parallel

• two-year, four-year, or five-year programs

☛ For more information: The National Commission for Cooperative Education

❑ Accelerated Degree

• degree earned in less than four academic years

❑ Three-Two Program

• three years liberal arts plus two years professional study

❑ External Degree

• up to 100% of credit may be earned in off-campus, non-traditional ways; average is about 50%

☛ For more information: *Bear's Guide to Earning Non-Traditional College Degrees*

❑ Off-campus study (U.S. or abroad), internships, exchanges — for credit

☛ For more information: *The Fiske Guide to Colleges*; The National Society for Internships and Experiential Education

❑ Honors

Sizes of Colleges and Universities

SMALL
- ❏ "small" is defined as under 2,500 students

  - over 1,000 schools have fewer than 1,000 students

  - under 1,000 schools have 1,000 - 2,500 students

- ❏ small classes

- ❏ easy access to faculty

- ❏ may have somewhat limited academic resources, extracurricular programs, and social activities unless near other colleges or a member of a college consortium

- ❏ often have strong community spirit

MEDIUM
- ❏ 2,500 - 5,000 students

  - about 500 schools have 2,500 - 5,000 students

  - under 400 schools have 5,000 - 10,000 students

LARGE
- ❏ over 10,000 students

  - about 320 schools have 10,000 - 30,000 students. Very few have 30,000 or more.

  - may have large introductory classes taught by teaching assistants or videos

- ❏ access to faculty varies

- ❏ offer wide variety of academic, extracurricular, and social activities

- ❏ keen competition for some extracurricular opportunities, such as varsity sports teams

FOUR-YEAR COLLEGES AND UNIVERSITIES

Most Selective

- ❏ approximately 50 colleges and universities accept fewer than 40% of those who apply

- ❏ a few colleges accept only 15%-20% of those who apply

- ❏ desirable criteria for admission: top 10% of class; 1250+ SAT's or 29+ ACT's; A grades; 3.5 - 4.0 GPA

Very Selective

- ❏ fewer than 200 colleges accept 40%-60% of those who apply

- ❏ desirable criteria for admission: top 20% - 30% of class; 1150+ SAT's or 26+ ACT's; A and B grades; 3.0 - 3.5 GPA

Somewhat Selective

- ❏ more than 1,000 colleges accept 60%-85% of those who apply

- ❏ desirable criteria for admission: top 50% of class; 900+ SAT's or 19+ ACT's; B and C grades; 2.0 - 3.0 GPA

Minimally Selective

- ❏ at least 270 colleges accept 85%-95% of those who apply

- ❏ acceptable criteria for admission: bottom 50% of class; 750-900 SAT's or 18 or below ACT's; C and D grades; 1.8 - 2.0 GPA

Non-Competitive

- ❏ at least 200 colleges accept all who apply ("open admissions")

- ❏ usually require high school diploma or equivalent

TWO-YEAR COLLEGES

❑ more than 1,200 two-year colleges

❑ most are minimally selective or have open admissions

❑ some are selective for certain programs or
require particular talents for admission

Costs:

Bear in mind that
paying for college
means more than
paying for tuition.
Other costs include:

✔ *Non-refundable application fees (usually $10-$50)*
✔ *Mandatory fees - (i.e. science lab fees,
darkroom fees for photography courses,
student government fees, etc.)*
✔ *Books and supplies*
✔ *Computer and software (if applicable)*
✔ *Room and board*
✔ *Other (costs of pre-admissions visits,
travel, insurance, phone, clothes,
entertainment, incidentals)*

TUITION

❑ Costs at both public and private colleges have been increasing
at an annual rate of approximately 6% - 9% and can be
expected to continue to increase in the near future.

❑ Tuition at public colleges is lower for in-state students than
for out-of-state students.

❑ Tuition for out-of-state students at public colleges is sometimes
higher than tuition at private colleges.

❑ "Comprehensive fees" include tuition, room, board, and mandatory
fees. These fees range from less than $5,000 to more than $20,000.

> **Lowest Costs**
> *Part-time semester-hour tuitions range from less than $50 to a few hundred dollars.*
>
> *U.S. military academies and at least one other college charge no tuition.*
>
> **Highest Costs**
> *Full-time tuition at some of the most selective private colleges is more than $12,000 a year.*

MANDATORY FEES

❑   may be less than $100 or over $1,000.

BOOKS AND SUPPLIES

❑   Costs vary, depending on courses taken, from a few hundred dollars to $1,000 or more.

❑   Costs may often be reduced by buying and selling used books in the college bookstore.

COMPUTER HARDWARE AND SOFTWARE

❑   required by some colleges and considered very desirable at others

❑   costs may run between $1,000 and $3,000

❑   some colleges offer student discount rates

ROOM AND BOARD

❑   On-campus costs range from a few thousand dollars to more than $5,000; room-only costs are comparably less.

❑   Costs may be less if you are living at home or off-campus.

Consortia and Special Programs

Many colleges expand opportunities and/or resources for students by developing joint programs with other colleges, such as off-campus study, cross-registration for classes, or semester exchange visits. Some of the best-known programs are

❏ **The Associated Colleges of the Mid-West**: off-campus study — overseas or U.S. (13 colleges, Mid-West)

❏ **The Christian College Consortium**: semester exchange visits (13 colleges; U.S.)

❏ **The Claremont Colleges Consortium**: shared services, cross registration, joint opportunities (5 colleges, California)

❏ **The Five College Consortium**: cross registration, use of libraries, social and cultural exchanges (5 colleges, Massachusetts)

❏ **The Great Lakes Colleges Association**: off-campus study overseas or in U.S. (12 colleges, Mid-West)

❏ **The Lehigh Valley Association of Independent Colleges**: inter-library loans, cultural programs, some cross-registration, study abroad (6 colleges, Pennsylvania)

❏ **Semester at Sea**: study on a ship and in twelve foreign countries for college credit (based at University of Pittsburgh)

❏ **The Seven-College Exchange**: exchange visits, foreign study programs, shared resources (7 colleges, Virginia)

❏ **The Southern College/University Union**: summer study programs in London (8 colleges, Southeast)

❏ **The Twelve-College Exchange Program**: one or two-semester exchange visits (12 colleges, Northeast)

❏ **The Washington Semester of American University:** academic and political opportunities (192 affiliated schools)

❏ **The Worcester Consortium**: shared resources, cross registration, special programs (10 colleges, Massachusetts)

❏ **The Venture Program:** college leave of absence for paid, temporary employment (6 colleges, Northeast)

☛ For further information:
The Fiske Guide to Colleges

Chapter III:

What Do Colleges Consider for Admission?

What Do Colleges Consider for Admission?

Most colleges consider a blend of academic and personal qualifications. Some consider academic qualifications only.

❑ Almost all colleges require a high school transcript and diploma. Many accept a General Educational Development (GED) certificate. Requirements may be waived for some students (over 25, senior citizens).

❑ The more selective the college, the more stringent the admissions requirements.

❑ Requirements at a college may differ for different programs or different students.

❑ Some colleges suggest criteria for admissions, such as SAT or ACT scores in a certain range, specific academic courses, and GPA's above some level.

❑ Colleges that require standardized tests usually like a balance between verbal and math scores. Very unbalanced scores should be explainable (e.g. learning disability) and appropriate for the college (e.g. high math scores for engineering).

A cademic qualifications are indicated by

- high school courses — substance, diversity, and level of difficulty

- high school grades, including senior year

- trends in grades (steady improvement, strong 11th grade record desirable)

- relationship of grades to standardized test scores (high scores and poor grades undesirable)

- rank in class

- standardized test scores

- academic honors and awards

- recommendations from guidance counselor and teachers

P ersonal qualifications are indicated by

- extracurricular activities, interests, and hobbies (most important for the very selective colleges)

- long-term commitment and talent in a few activities (e.g. sports, arts, student government, community service)

- recommendations from guidance counselor, one or two teachers, possibly an employer or a close friend — people who know you well and appreciate your strengths and your potential

- application essays

- personal interviews

Other Considerations

- relationship to alumnus(a) (One who is influential or a generous donor can help).

- siblings at the college (especially if they are/were successful students)

- geographic, ethnic, sex, socio-economic representation needed to balance a class

- number of applicants from your high school

- reputation of your high school

Guide to Academic Criteria for Admission*

	MOST SELECTIVE	VERY SELECTIVE	SOMEWHAT SELECTIVE	MINIMALLY SELECTIVE
Courses in High School	4 English 3-4 Math 3 Science 3-4 Foreign Language 3+ Social Studies 5-6 Academic courses/year AP, Honors courses Electives in Art, Music, Computer	4 English 3 Math 3 Science 3-4 Foreign Language 3 Social Studies 5 Academic courses/year AP, Honors courses Electives in Art, Music, Computer	3-4 English 3 Math 2 Science 2 Foreign Language Academic and/or general course diploma	3 English Some math and science General or basic course diploma
Grades	Mostly A's	Mostly A's and B's	Mostly B's and C's	Mostly C's
Grade Point Average (GPA)	3.5 - 4.0	3.0 - 3.5	2.0 - 3.0	1.8 - 2.0
Rank in Class	Top 10%	Top 20%-30%	Top 50%	Bottom 50%
Standardized Tests Required	SAT's or ACT's 3+ Achievements, including English 2+ AP's	SAT's or ACT's 2+ Achievements, including English 1-2+ AP's	SAT's or ACT's Sometimes required, sometimes only recommended 0-2 Achievements	SAT's, ACT's usually not required, but used for counseling and placement No Achievements required
Standardized Test Scores	1250+ SAT's or 29+ ACT's 650+ Achievements 4+ AP's	1150+ SAT's or 26+ ACT's 550+ Achievements 3+ AP's	900+ SAT's or 19+ ACT's	750-900 SAT's 18 or below ACT's

These criteria are desirable or acceptable, but not essential. Many factors are considered in making admissions decisions.

Chapter IV:

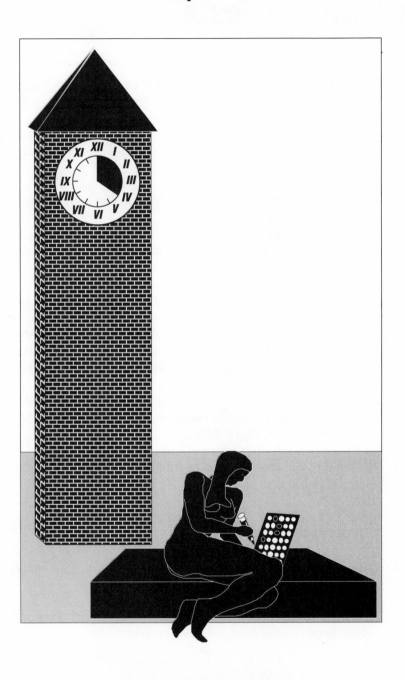

Standardized Tests

Standardized Tests

❑ These tests are required by the "most selective" and "very selective" colleges, and by some "somewhat selective" colleges.

❑ They are not required by "minimally selective" colleges, but it's a good idea to take them while you're still in high school in case you need the scores later.

❑ Make your best effort on these tests. Don't be complacent.

❑ The best source of information about all the tests, test dates, and preparation is your high school guidance office, where free booklets should be available.

✓ Contact the College Board Admissions Testing Program (ATP) for information about Preliminary Scholastic Aptitude Tests (PSAT's), Scholastic Aptitude Tests (SAT's), Achievement Tests, Advanced Placement Tests (AP's), Test of English as a Foreign Language (TOEFL), or College-Level Examination Program (CLEP).

✓ Contact the ACT National Office for information about P-ACT+, American College Testing Program (ACT's), and the Proficiency Examination Program (PEP).

❑ ATP and ACT tests may be taken at test centers throughout the United States.

❑ Both the ATP and ACT tests change periodically. Be sure to use up-to-date information.

❑ Many colleges accept either the SAT's or the ACT's. Test results are sent only to the colleges you designate.

❑ SAT's and Achievement Tests must be scheduled on separate test dates.

The best source of information about all the tests, test dates, and preparation is your high school guidance office, where free booklets should be available.

❏ Regular registration deadlines for tests are approximately six weeks before test dates.

❏ All tests have registration fees. These can be waived if you can't afford to pay. See your high school guidance counselor for information.

❏ Late registration is possible for SAT's and ACT's, for additional fees. Stand-by registration is possible for SAT's but not for ACT's.

❏ When scheduling tests, allow at least six weeks for colleges to receive test results before application deadlines. Rush score reporting is available but costly.

❏ For information about such matters as cancelling test scores, obtaining score reports, or sending rush reports to colleges, consult the free test booklets.

❏ For both the testing services (ATP and ACT), Sunday testing is available for religious reasons. Private or special testing is available for handicapped students, students with learning disabilities, or others with unusual circumstances. These special tests are arranged by your school and must be documented. Taking these tests, when appropriate, probably does not hurt your chances for admission.
☛ For more information: ATP Services for Handicapped Students or ACT Test Administration

Information about the standardized tests most commonly used in the admissions process and about preparation for these tests begins on the next page.

The Tests

PRELIMINARY SCHOLASTIC APTITUDE TEST (PSAT) / NATIONAL MERIT SCHOLARSHIP QUALIFYING TEST (NMSQT)

❏ The PSAT is a "practice test" for the SAT. It is a shortened version of the SAT with verbal and mathematical reasoning sections.

> ✓ *For 11th grade students, the PSAT is also used to select for National Merit Scholarships and for the National Achievement Scholarship Program for Outstanding Negro Students.*

❏ It is usually taken in October of the 11th grade, but may also be taken in the 10th grade. Scores, which range from 200 to 800 on each section, usually go on your high school transcript, although they can be omitted. They may be sent to colleges but are not used for college admissions. Consult your guidance counselor or PSAT/NMSQT for more information.

❏ The registration form for the PSAT contains a Student Descriptive Questionnaire. Completion is voluntary. If you complete it, be aware that what you say may "label" you, and you may receive materials from a variety of colleges.

P—ACT+

❏ This test is coordinated with the ACT's. It emphasizes college preparatory skills. It also aids in course selection and in college and career planning.

❏ The academic tests measure knowledge and skills in writing, mathematics, reading, and science reasoning, not aptitude.

❏ Scores range from 1 to 36. They may go on your high school transcript but are not used in college admissions.

❏ The P-ACT+ is usually given in the fall of 10th grade.

SCHOLASTIC APTITUDE TESTS (SAT'S)

- ❏ SAT's have a verbal section (reading comprehension and vocabulary), a math section (problem-solving), one experimental section on which you are not scored, and a test of standard written English (TSWE) scored separately and used primarily for placement in college English classes, not for college admissions.

- ❏ Scores on the verbal and math sections range from 200 to 800 each. Recent national average scores were verbal 430 and math 476.

- ❏ Scores are usually higher on the SAT's than on the PSAT's. All SAT scores go to the colleges to which you're applying.

- ❏ You may take the SAT's three times or more, but in most cases twice is enough. The higher the score, the harder it is to improve it. And remember, *all* of your scores are sent to the colleges.

- ❏ Some colleges consider only your highest score. Others take averages or look at the total score picture.

AMERICAN COLLEGE TESTS (ACT'S)

- ❏ The ACT's are commonly used for admission to colleges in the Southeast, Mid-West and Mountain Plains states. It is the dominant testing program in 28 states.

- ❏ Tests cover four academic subject areas: English, Mathematics, Reading, and Science Reasoning.

- ❏ ACT's test problem-solving and reasoning skills in relation to academic subjects. ACT's do not test aptitude.

- ❏ Composite scores range from 1 to 36.

- ❏ Mean composite score for college-bound students is about 18; a strong score is 25 or more.

✏ ACHIEVEMENT TESTS

❏ These are one-hour, multiple choice tests in specific academic areas: American History and Social Studies; Biology; Chemistry; English Composition (with or without essay); European History and World Cultures; French; German; Modern Hebrew; Italian; Latin; Literature; Math Level I (primarily algebra and geometry); Math Level II (includes trigonometry and elementary functions); Physics; Spanish.

❏ One or more Achievements is required by many colleges. Check carefully which tests these are. Three are usually enough, although you may take more.

❏ Take optional Achievement Tests only if you think you'll do well. Poor scores may hurt your chances for admission. Ask your guidance counselor and teachers which tests are appropriate for you.

❏ Some Achievement Tests are given only on certain test dates. Check carefully.

❏ The English Composition test with essay is recommended by some colleges. It is given only once a year, in December.

✏ ADVANCED PLACEMENT TESTS (AP'S)

❏ These multiple-choice, free-response tests, based on college-level high school courses, are given in Art, Music, English, Economics, Government and Politics, History, French, German, Latin, Spanish, Biology, Chemistry, Physics, Calculus, and Computer Science.

 Many colleges grant college credit for AP scores of 3 or higher. With a sufficient number of such credits (determined by each college), it may be possible to attain sophomore standing upon entering college.

❏ You may take AP tests even if you haven't completed an AP course.

❏ These are important for the "most selective" and "very selective" colleges.

❏ AP scores are sent to your colleges only if you request it.

❏ Scores range from 1 to 5.

☛ For more information: AP Program; AP Services

TEST OF ENGLISH AS A FOREIGN LANGUAGE (TOEFL)

❑　Tests foreign students or non-English-speaking students to determine fluency in English.

❑　Required by many colleges for foreign applicants.

☛ For more information:　TOEFL

COLLEGE-LEVEL EXAMINATION PROGRAM (CLEP)

❑　Taken to get college credit for "out-of-school" learning. Credits are granted by a college, not by the College Board ATP.

❑　Tests include general examinations and subject exams in Composition and Literature, Foreign Language, History and Social Sciences, Science and Mathematics, and Business.

☛ For more information:　*CLEP: The College Board Guide to CLEP Examinations*

PROFICIENCY EXAMINATION PROGRAM (PEP)

❑　These tests are taken to get college credit for "out-of-school" learning. Credits are granted by a college, not by the American College Testing Program (ACT).

❑　Tests are given in more than 40 course subjects, in the areas of Arts and Sciences, Business, Education, and Nursing.

☛ For more information and study guides:　ACT PEP.

DANTES/SUBJECT STANDARDIZED TESTS

❑　Tests to get college credit for "out-of-school" learning. Credits are granted by a college, not by the Educational Testing Service.

- ❏ Tests are given in Applied Technology, Business, Languages, Mathematics, Science, and Social Science areas.

  ☛ For more information: Educational Testing Service.

Preparation for Standardized Tests

- ❏ Some preparation is advisable, particularly in test-taking techniques.

- ❏ Whatever the preparation, there is no guarantee that your scores will improve.

BEST PREPARATION

- ❏ rigorous course study throughout school

- ❏ lifetime reading of challenging books, magazines, and newspapers

- ❏ review related course content, when appropriate (e.g. AP's, algebra and geometry for Math SAT's and Math Level 1 Achievement Test)

- ❏ use free practice test booklets for PSAT's, SAT's, P-ACT+'s, ACT's, and Achievement Tests. These should be available in your guidance office.

OTHER PREPARATION

- ❏ Use practice test books such as *10 SAT's* and *The College Board Achievement Tests*. These books include actual, recently-administered tests. They are available in bookstores or from The College Board.

- *Princeton Review's Cracking the System: The SAT*

- *Gruber's Complete Preparation for the SAT*

- *Up Your SAT Score,* probably the most fun test preparation book you'll find.

- Peterson's *SAT Panic Plan* & *SAT Success*

- The College Board's video "Taking the SAT"

- "College Pursuit," a game

COURSES

- Stanley H. Kaplan Educational Centers offer classes, audio tapes, and home study materials in more than 120 locations in the United States. For information, phone (800) KAP-TEST.

- The Princeton Review offers courses and tutoring in many regions of the United States. Phone (800) 333-0369 for information and locations.

- Many local high schools, community colleges, and private individuals offer preparation courses. Check with your guidance counselor, read newspaper ads, consult your phone book, and ask acquaintances.

COMPUTER PROGRAMS

- These may be expensive, although there are some for about $50. Ask your guidance counselor about available school-owned programs to be used at school or borrowed for home use.

- Useful if you'd prefer to take sample tests on a computer screen rather than with pencil and paper.

- Two programs are available from The College Board: "Test Sense: Preparing For the PSAT/NMSQT" and "Test Wise: Preparing For the SAT."

Standardized Tests — Personal Notes

Use this page to note important dates, scores, etc.

Chapter V:

Getting Started:
What Do You Need in a College?

Getting Started:
What Do You Need in a College?

Before you choose specific colleges to which you might apply, think about yourself and what a college must offer to meet your needs.

Thinking About Yourself

YOUR ACADEMIC RECORD

❑ courses taken

❑ high school grades

❑ standardized test scores (SAT's, ACT's, Achievements, AP's)

❑ class rank

❑ awards or honors

YOUR STRONG INTERESTS AND IMPORTANT ACTIVITIES

❑ school — athletics, arts, publications, leadership

❑ non-school — work, volunteer, hobbies

❑ summers — work, courses, travel, volunteer

YOU AS A STUDENT

❑ academic likes and dislikes: favorite subjects and least favorite subjects; research interests

❑ academic skills: strengths and weaknesses in abstract reasoning, reading, writing, problem solving, creativity

❏   attitudes and habits:

Are you:
✓ naturally curious or mostly indifferent?
✓ a hard worker or a "coaster"?
✓ well organized or disorganized?
✓ an active participant or quiet in your classes?
✓ a good test-taker or a poor test-taker?

Do you:
✓ have good relationships with teachers or not very much contact?
✓ enjoy reading, writing, researching, and studying or tend to avoid these ?
✓ work well under pressure or prefer a relaxed academic setting?

YOUR PERSONAL CHARACTERISTICS

Are you:
✓ an independent experience-seeker or do you prefer to play it safe?

Do you:
✓ like a diversity of people or people more like yourself?
✓ have liberal or conservative attitudes about politics and behavior?
✓ have any special health needs or other limitations?
✓ like lots of privacy or prefer to be with people?

YOUR LONG-TERM GOALS

❏   graduate school

❏   career

❏   life-style

YOUR IMAGE

❏   How do people who know you well (parents, close friends, teachers) rate your interests, skills, and characteristics? Ask them!

College Criteria to Consider — A Checklist

Criteria	Very Important (Definitely Want)	Fairly Important (Probably Want)	Unimportant (Doesn't Matter)	Not Sure
Type of College				
2-year college				
4-year college				
University				
Public school				
Private school				
Military academy				
Program				
Liberal Arts				
Occupational/ Pre-professional				
Comprehensive				
Specialized/ Single-purpose				
Selectivity				
Most selective				
Very selective				
Somewhat selective				
Minimally selective				
Non-competitive				
Faculty				
Large % with Ph.D's				
Low faculty/ student ratio				
Accessibility				
Comprehensive Cost				
As low as possible				
Less than $7,000 a year				
More than $7,000 a year				

Criteria	Very Important (Definitely Want)	Fairly Important (Probably Want)	Unimportant (Doesn't Matter)	Not Sure
Size				
Small				
Medium				
Large				
Location				
Northeast				
Mid-Atlantic				
South				
Mid-West				
West				
Urban				
Suburban				
Rural				
Close to home				
Easy access by car, plane, train, or bus				
Student body				
Coed				
Single sex				
Diverse				
Homogeneous				
Liberal				
Conservative				
Resident				
Commuter				
Large % under 25				
Large % over 25				
Large % on financial aid				
Small % on financial aid				
Religion				
Strong emphasis				
Minimal emphasis				

Criteria	Very Important (Definitely Want)	Fairly Important (Probably Want)	Unimportant (Doesn't Matter)	Not Sure
Requirements for graduation				
Numerous required courses				
Core curriculum				
Flexible course choice				
Traditional majors				
Self-designed majors				
Academic Atmosphere				
Competitive				
Non-competitive				
Intense				
Relaxed				
Scholarly				
Career-oriented				
Campus Activity				
Lots of parties				
Low-key				
Strong fraternity/ sorority system				
Excellent varsity sports				
Intramural sports				
Cultural opportunities				

Criteria	Very Important (Definitely Want)	Fairly Important (Probably Want)	Unimportant (Doesn't Matter)	Not Sure
Campus				
Beauty				
Guaranteed housing for freshmen				
Housing available for all students				
Quality academic facilities				
Excellent sports facilities				
Excellent arts facilities				
Handicap access				
Well-equipped library				
Large — spread out				
Small — self-contained				
Special Programs				
Accelerated degree				
External degree				
Three-two program				
Internships				
Co-op jobs				
Cross-registration				
Exchange programs				
Study abroad				
Honors				
ROTC				
Health, counseling services				
Remedial, LD, ESL services				

What I Want in a College — Personal Notes

Use this page to note your preferences, needs, etc.

Chapter VI:

Making Your List

Making Your List

Once you've thought hard about yourself and your college needs, it's time to start thinking about specific colleges and to make a list of those to which you might apply.

February of 11th grade is a good time to begin.

Preliminary List

❏ Review the college criteria that are most important to you. Select two or three that are top priority, such as the type of academic program and location.

❏ Get one or more objective, comprehensive college guidebooks or directories. Look in your school guidance office, bookstore, public library, or borrow from friends. Some reputable guidebooks include

Barron's Profiles of American Colleges
The College Handbook
Comparative Guide to American Colleges
G.I.S. Guide to Four-Year Colleges
Peterson's Guide to Four-Year Colleges
Peterson's Guide to Two-Year Colleges
The Right College
ACT's College Planning/Search Book

❏ Using the guidebook(s), start a list of colleges or universities that are appropriate and meet the two or three high priority criteria that you have decided upon.

❏ Check indexes in the guidebook(s). You will find colleges and universities listed by categories, such as majors and career choices, location, entrance difficulties, cost ranges, ROTC programs, vital statistics, etc.

❏ Don't rule out any college because it doesn't offer a particular major. Graduate schools usually accept a wide variety of majors. You may be able to design your own.

- ❏ Don't rule out any college because it doesn't offer a particular "study abroad" or other off-campus program. Many colleges will accept a program you find on your own.

- ❏ Get suggestions from people who know you and know about colleges, such as your high school guidance counselor, teachers, family members, and acquaintances.

- ❏ Start with a long list (30 or more schools) and plan to narrow it later.

 If you have definite career goals, seek colleges strong in that field. Remember, you might change your mind. If you do not have definite goals, seek colleges with a wide range of offerings.

- ❏ If you're in doubt about the credentials of colleges or programs, check with your state higher education agency. Call (800) 333-INFO for address and phone number. See *Bear's Guide to Earning Non-Traditional College Degrees* for a list of recognized accrediting agencies.

- ❏ All colleges on your preliminary list should be reasonably appropriate as far as entrance selectivity is concerned. As a guideline, your SAT scores should be within 200 points of the average score for the schools you are considering.

- ❏ If a particular sport is your strong point, determine which colleges predominate in that sport and might be interested in you as a member of the team. Start by asking your coaches.
  ☞ For further information: *Going the Distance, NCAA Guide for the College Bound Student Athlete,* and *The Winning Edge: A Complete Guide to Intercollegiate Athletic Programs.*

- ❏ If you are an average or above-average student, look at guidebooks such as: *The Fiske Guide to Colleges; The Insider's Guide to Colleges; Peterson's Competitive Colleges; Barron's Guide to the Most Prestigious Colleges; The Public Ivys; How To Get an Ivy League Education at a State University.*

- ❏ If you are interested in highly ranked colleges, consult the latest edition of the U.S. News' *America's Best Colleges.*

- ❏ If you are interested in highly ranked programs, consult the latest edition of *The Gourman Report*, which lists the most highly rated programs in more than 100 separate educational fields in over 1,000 colleges and universities, or *Rugg's Recommendations on the Colleges.*

- ❏ Talk with college representatives who visit your high school for "college night" or at other times throughout the year. Attend local college fairs. Prepare yourself (appropriate appearance and questions) as you would for a formal interview, as these representatives may read your application and remember you.

- ❏ Make preliminary visits to a few types of nearby schools (large state university, small private college) to get an idea about what type you might like.

- ❏ Ask your guidance counselor about the availability of a free college choice computer program, such as Guidance Information Services (GIS), College Board's *College Explorer*, or ACT's *Educational Opportunity Service* (EOS)–you may get some ideas. Consider carefully whether it's worth paying for a service such as Peterson's *College Quest* or Octameron's *College Selection Service.*

- ❏ Consider using ACT's *Discover*, a career exploration and educational planning system that offers computerized programs for students of all ages.

- ❏ Ask your guidance counselor about taking the Armed Services Vocational Aptitude Battery (ASVAB). You may get ideas about your college and career planning. The test is free — there's no obligation.

- ❏ Also ask your guidance counselor about the availability of free video cassettes and films, such as the College Board's *College Choice/Student Choice*. These may help you choose a college, help you with your application, or give you information about individual colleges. Videos about individual.colleges may be ordered directly from Peterson's College Video Library for a fee.

- ❏ Consider hiring a college consultant. For information and a list of professional college consultants, write The Independent Educational Consultants Association (IECA) or The National Association of College Admissions Counselors. Since many competent educational consultants do not belong to IECA, consult the yellow pages, read ads in your local newspaper, and ask acquaintances. Before you hire a college consultant, find out what the service and costs will be, and ask for references. Expect confidentiality, objectivity, and a good list of suggestions of appropriate colleges for you. Don't expect miracles — consultants cannot guarantee admission or success in college.

Narrowing Your List

In your 11th grade spring semester, narrow your list to no more than 20 appropriate colleges. To help you do this, select two or three additional criteria that are very important to you — e. g. housing availability, high percent of students of your race or ethnic origin, availability of a particular varsity sport, etc. Then:

1. Scan college profiles in comprehensive guidebooks, eliminating colleges that don't meet your most important, essential criteria. Read in-depth descriptions, if available, in comprehensive guidebooks and/or *The Fiske Guide to Colleges, The Insider's Guide,* and *The Public Ivys.*

2. Look for indicators of quality: accreditation information; test scores and class rank of students accepted; percent of faculty with doctoral or advanced degrees; percent of graduates admitted to graduate schools; percent of entering students who graduate; large endowments; and strong financial support.

3. Send for information. Mail a post card or brief letter requesting a catalog, viewbook, profile of the most recent freshman class, application, and, if desired, financial aid forms, to each of the colleges remaining on your list. (This request should be neatly written and grammatically correct, as it will probably go into your college folder).

As you receive materials, organize them in boxes or files. Place application and financial aid forms where you can easily find them.

❏   Glance at the photos in the view books and brochures, but be aware that these are advertisements to "sell" the colleges.

❏   Check admissions requirements (Are you eligible?), graduation requirements (Are these reasonable for you?), and academic and extracurricular offerings (Do they offer the courses and activities you want?).

❏   Start a notebook with a page or two for each college that interests you. Record application due dates and the pros and cons of each college.

Chapter VII:

Deciding Where You Will Apply:
Campus Visits and Interviews

Deciding Where You Will Apply: Campus Visits and Interviews

You'll probably want to apply to at least six colleges: two "long shots"; two "possibles"; and two "good bets." You may add a few more (ten should be plenty) or you may apply to fewer than six if your needs are very specific. If possible, visit the colleges you are considering and arrange personal interviews, if offered and/or required. If on-campus interviews aren't available, ask about interviews with college representatives in your area.

Campus Visits

❑ Phone the colleges at least three weeks in advance (many have toll free numbers) to make appointments for group tours and group or personal interviews. Group interviews are information sessions for students and parents.
Ask about the best and worst times to visit each college.
Allow about 45 minutes for each personal interview.

❑ Some colleges have special days for prospective students. Ask about these.

 Arrange 12th-grade, fall semester, on-campus personal interviews at least 2-3 months in advance.

❑ Don't expect to get an interview at the last moment. If you do have an appointment, be there on time.

❑ It isn't necessary to talk to the Director or Dean of Admissions. Any admissions interviewer is fine.

❑ As you visit, record information and impressions in your notebook.

✓ **For practice, visit and arrange an interview at a nearby college that you may not attend.**

❑ Go with a friend or two, with or without parents.

❑ Visit while the college is in session, if possible.

❑ Visit no more than three colleges in one day, preferably only one or two.

❑ Make arrangements in advance if you want to talk to an athletic coach or a faculty member in a particular department, to sit in on classes, to stay in dorms overnight, etc.

❑ In the admissions office, ask for a course catalog and a profile of students, if these haven't been sent to you. Ask about realistic college costs. Look at the yearbook.

❑ Take a group tour *before* your interview.

❑ Visit the library and the student center. Talk with students.

❑ Sample a meal in the cafeteria.

❑ Look at bulletin boards. What's happening on campus?

❑ Read the college newspaper. What are the issues?

❑ Look in the bookstore for a student evaluation of courses and faculty.

❑ Try not to be too influenced by the weather during your visit or by the particular admissions person or student guide you meet.

❑ Explore living conditions. Are the dorms overcrowded? Are there lounges? Where and what do students eat?

❑ Are there quiet places to study? How easy is it to get around the campus? What is there is to do on weekends?

Interviews

BEFORE THE INTERVIEW

❑   Take the group tour.

❑   Review basic facts about the college.

❑   Plan how you'll obtain additional information at the interview and how you'll emphasize your strong points and unique qualifications.

❑   Plan several questions you'd really like to ask, such as the quality of a particular department or the extent of career advising.

❑   Be prepared to talk about things you've done so far, your future plans, and why you think this particular college would meet your needs.

❑   Be aware of major current political and social issues.

❑   Unless you have already sent your application, bring a copy of your transcript with you, as well as any supporting materials that make you unique.

❑   Remember that your dress and appearance will make an impression.

DURING THE INTERVIEW

❑   The interviewer will introduce himself or herself. Remember this person's name.

❑   The interviewer will probably ask you several questions and then give you a chance to ask your own questions.

❑   Be honest. Relax and act natural.

❑   Keep eye contact with the interviewer.

❑   Don't discuss your standardized test scores or any negative part of your record unless you're asked.

❑   Don't ask factual questions that can be found in the catalog or other college materials.

❑   At the end of the interview, it's OK to ask about your chances for admission.

☛ For more tips on interviews, consult *Campus Pursuit: How To Make the Most of the College Visit and Interview; Campus Visits and College Interviews*

AFTER THE INTERVIEW

❑   Write a thank you note to your interviewer. Include any additional questions you may have.

DECISIONS

✓   Review all the information you've gathered during visits and interviews.

✓   Record information, impressions, and feelings in your notebook.

✓   Make your final decisions about where you will apply.

Campus Visits and Interviews — Personal Notes

Use this page to note your preferences, tricky interview questions, etc.

Chapter VIII:

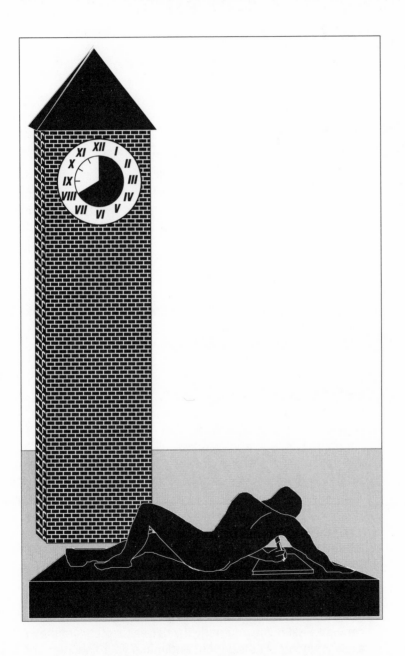

Applications and Final College Choice

Applications and Final College Choice

Preliminary Decisions

Decide by fall semester of 11th grade whether you want to apply for Early Entrance, or by October of 12th grade for Early Decision or Early Action. Do your chosen colleges offer these options? What are the deadlines for these applications?

O   **Early Entrance**
Some colleges offer admission before you graduate from high school. Consider this only if you are a mature, highly qualified, 11th grade or beginning 12th grade student.

O   **Early Decision**
Early Decision means you apply early to a single college, you are notified early, usually in December, and if accepted, you agree to attend that college and withdraw all other applications. Consider this option if there is one college you prefer over all the rest and you think your chances of acceptance are very good. Applying Early Decision demonstrates your strong commitment to the college and may be an advantage in the admissions process. If you are not accepted, your application may be considered again in the regular admissions process. You will still have time to apply to other colleges.

O   **Early Action**
A few of the most selective colleges allow you to apply early and will notify you early if you're accepted, yet they still allow you to apply elsewhere and make your final decision in May. However, if you're rejected, your application may not be considered in the regular application process.

General Tips on Applications

✎ In September of 12th grade, see your guidance counselor about your high school's application procedures and deadlines. Check your transcript for accuracy. Be sure honors courses are listed. Find out if your counselor plans to write a letter of recommendation.

✔ ***Send applications as early as possible. Your application will get more careful attention, and you'll be less likely to lose out on housing and financial aid.***

✎ If you consider applying for financial aid, find out if your college choices have "need blind" admissions policies (that is, your financial status has no bearing on whether you are accepted or rejected) or if your financial aid application will affect admissions decisions.

✎ File financial aid applications separately with the financial aid offices. Send these even earlier than the regular admissions applications, if possible.

✎ If an application comes in two parts, send Part I (usually just basic information) immediately so your file can be started. Don't procrastinate.

✎ Applications to colleges with "rolling admissions" may be sent up to a year before you would enter. A few weeks after sending those applications, you will be notified of acceptance or rejection, but you can usually wait until the regular reply date to make your decision. Check with the colleges.

✎ Make copies of all application forms to use as rough drafts. Save the official copies to complete and mail to the colleges.

✎ More than 100 private colleges accept a **Common Application** form. Ask the Admissions Offices if they accept it. The **Common Application** will save you time and stress, but you might prefer to complete the colleges' own forms, as these may give you more opportunity to personalize your applications.

✎ A few colleges have computerized application systems. Ask the Admissions Offices.

❏ **_When filling out the applications:_**

✍ Follow directions exactly.

✍ Be honest, thorough and realistic. Don't be overly modest or overly boastful. Don't try to disguise your true self to "fit" the college.

✍ Type, if possible, or write legibly. Cover errors neatly with white-out.

✍ Use correct spelling and grammar.

✍ Avoid glaring mistakes, such as selecting a major that isn't offered.

✍ Feel free to be "undecided" about your major, especially for liberal arts colleges.

✍ If you do declare a major, be sure it is consistent with the rest of your application (grades, scores, essay).

✍ List your most important activities and hobbies first, and list only those to which you've made a strong commitment.

✍ Anything you can do to show that you're a curious, motivated student will be helpful.

✍ Anything you can do to show that you intend to graduate from that college will be helpful.

✍ If asked to list other schools to which you are applying, list only 4 or 5 realistic choices. Your choices can say a lot about you.

✍ Use white, unlined, good quality paper for any additional pages to your application.

✍ If you send a photo, a flattering, "head and shoulders" color snapshot is best.

✍ Sending a creative "gimmick"— such as a video or homemade cookies — may help your application stand out, but it must be excellent, or it may come across as silly and irrelevant.

✍ If you have some truly top quality material that shows your talent in your strong interest area, send it with your application (e.g. a tape of a solo concert performance or a short story published in a magazine).

Writing the Essay

✍ Essays can be very important. Plan to spend time and effort.

✍ There are no "right" or "wrong" essays. Essays are simply your opportunity to tell the colleges more about yourself.

✍ Allow at least two weeks from first outline to final draft. Get started early. Jot down ideas as they occur to you. Don't put off the actual writing. The thought of writing is often much worse than actually doing it.

✍ Before you start writing, note instructions as to length and preferred printing (hand written, typed, word processed).

✍ Read each essay question carefully. Think about what you can say that will answer that particular question and, at the same time, make you stand out as an individual.

✍ Think about emphasizing one or more strong academic, extracurricular, or personal interests that you have presented elsewhere in your application, but don't just repeat what you've already said.

T *he essay may be your only chance to describe the "real you" to the admissions committee. Don't blow it by being pompous, dull, or childish. Use the essay to give the committee a reason to admit you, not reject you.*

✍ Consider how you will present your interests and strengths as an asset to each particular college.

✍ Write an outline. Then write one or more rough drafts using your own words. Give specific examples to support general statements. Write no more than three pages, fewer if possible, unless otherwise instructed.

✍ Ask a few people (parent, teacher) to read your best draft and suggest ideas. Don't allow anyone else to do the writing.

✍ Revise your draft until you are satisfied. Be sure that spelling and grammar are *perfect*.

✍ Type (or write) your essay on a practice copy of the application form. Adjust the length, if necessary.

✍ Type or write your essay on the official application form. If using additional paper, be sure that it's good quality, white, and unlined.

☛ For more information — and inspiration — read *Essays That Worked: 50 Essays from Successful Applications to the Nation's Top Colleges.*

Letters of Recommendation

✉ Your school guidance counselor will probably write the school's recommendation. Make sure your counselor knows you personally, at least by spring semester, 11th grade.

✉ Send at least the number of recommendations suggested, but no more than one or two others.

✉ Ask for a recommendation from at least one teacher who will praise you as a student in your area of special interest.

✉ Ask for recommendations early. Give plenty of time (at least two weeks). Provide any forms sent by colleges, as well as stamped, addressed envelopes.

☒ Waive your legal rights to see the recommendations.

☒ Ask for a recommendation from a non-school employer, supervisor, or teacher who will emphasize your personal strengths, such as dependability or creativity.

☒ Letters from alumni, influential family members, or your own close friends sometimes help.

☒ Don't bother with general letters from family friends.

☒ Check later to be sure that the letters have been sent.

☒ Thank each person who has written a recommendation for you.

Final Tips On Applications

✓ If your application does not require an essay, send a brief cover letter explaining why you're applying to that college. Include any important information that doesn't appear elsewhere in the application. Explain, if possible, without apologizing, anything unusual, such as a single low grade.

✓ Make and file copies of your finished applications before you mail the originals.

✓ Attach a check for the application fee.

✓ If you haven't received acknowledgment after about two weeks, phone the admissions offices and financial aid offices to be sure your applications are complete.

☛ For more information on applications: *Admit One! Your Guide to College Application; Your College Application.*

Final Choice

❏ Dates on which you will be notified of action on your applications vary. Colleges using "continuous" notification may notify you a few weeks after your applications have been submitted. Others wait until their published notification date. Within a given college, notification dates are different for Early Decision, regular, and transfer applicants. Reply dates also vary. Many colleges use the National Candidates Reply Date of May 1.

❏ If you receive more than one acceptance, review your college notebook for pros and cons.

❏ Discuss your choices with others: parent(s) and other family members, teachers, guidance counselor, alumni from your high school who attend or have recently attended those colleges.

❏ If you are accepted at a desirable college that you have not seen, try to visit before the reply date.

❏ If you've already visited, consider another visit and an overnight stay, if possible.

❏ If you're a strong applicant, don't be surprised if colleges try to entice you with special invitations and/or offers of no-need financial aid.

❏ Once accepted, you may want "deferred entrance" (entering college the following year). Ask an admissions officer if you need to reapply.

❏ If you are wait-listed at the college of your choice, write again to emphasize your desire to attend. Send any additional favorable information. Ask your guidance counselor to call about your chances. Don't make a nuisance of yourself by calling frequently. Send a deposit to reserve your place at one of the colleges at which you've been accepted, just in case.

❏ Make your final choice by the deadline. Send your deposit(s) and any requested information or materials.

❏ Notify, in writing, all other colleges where you have been accepted of your decision not to enroll.

Chapter IX:

Admissions Process Calendar

Admissions Process Calendar

8th and 9th Grades

❑ Think and talk about college in general, but not specific colleges.

❑ Think about how you and your family might finance your college education.

❑ Work on good study habits, organizational skills, and social skills.

❑ Take opportunities to be away from home.

❑ Read and write as much as possible.

❑ Take the most challenging courses you can manage and get the best grades possible.

❑ Continue developing skills and seek opportunities for independence.

❑ Develop two or three strong extracurricular interests, either in school or out of school.

10th Grade / Fall Semester

❑ Talk to your guidance counselor about the standardized testing schedule and your high school course selections. Plan to take the most challenging courses you can manage.

❑ If you plan to take ACT's, take the P-ACT+, if offered by your high school.

❑ If you plan to take SAT's, consider taking the Preliminary Scholastic Aptitude Test (PSAT) in October.

Think more specifically about financing your college education.
☛ For information, read a book such as *Don't Miss Out: The Ambitious Student's Guide to Financial Aid.*

❏   If available, attend "college night" or a local college fair in your community.

Summer before 11th Grade

❏   If possible, do something interesting and challenging: get a job, do volunteer work, travel, take a learning program.

❏   Consider a few preliminary college visits.

   ☛ For ideas: *Peterson's Summer Opportunities for Kids and Teenagers; Summer Options for Teenagers;* National Association of Independent School's *Boarding Schools: Special Programs;* American Camping Association's *Guide to Accredited Camps; Summer Jobs: Opportunities in the Federal Government.*

11th Grade / Fall Semester

❏   Be sure you have a Social Security number.

❏   Take the PSAT in October (scores come in December).

❏   If available, attend "college night" at your high school or a college fair in your community.

❏   Speak with college recruiters who visit your high school.

❏   If you're interested in Early Entrance or Early Decision or plan to apply to "most selective" or "very selective" colleges, take SAT's and Achievement Tests as needed. Proceed with application process.

11th Grade / Spring Semester

❏   In January or February, start thinking about ways to prepare for the SAT's or ACT's. Check registration deadlines.

❏   In February, begin to think about specific colleges and start your list. Later in the semester, narrow your list and send for preliminary information and applications.

❑ Be sure your guidance counselor knows you personally and knows your college plans.

❑ If you haven't done so, attend a "college night" or college fair.

❑ Take SAT's (March, May, or June) or ACT's (April).

❑ During spring vacation, start college visits. Take group tours but don't try for personal interviews.

❑ If applying to "most selective" or "very selective" colleges, you will probably want to take these Achievement Tests in May or June: Math Level I or II, English Composition, and one other, particularly in a strong subject (e.g. science, foreign language, or history).

❑ Take junior year Advanced Placement (AP) exams (May).

Summer before 12th Grade

❑ Complete college visits and interviews, especially if you're considering Early Decision.

❑ Arrange interviews for fall semester. Allow 2-3 months for appointments.

❑ Do something interesting and challenging.

❑ Consider a college summer program for high school students. Ask the colleges you're interested in if they have one. Check your high school guidance office for information. Consult *Summer on Campus: College Experiences for High School Students; A Taste of College: On-Campus Summer Programs for High School Students.*

❑ If you are undecided about your future goals, consider some career counseling. Ask your guidance counselor for suggestions.

❑ Send for college applications in late summer to get an early start.

12th Grade / Fall Semester

❑ Decide where you'll apply. Send for catalogs, viewbooks, and application forms that you don't have. Ask for a profile of the most recent freshmen class.

❑ See your guidance counselor. Check your transcript for accuracy. Find out if your guidance counselor will send a letter of recommendation with your transcript.

❑ Continue visits and interviews. If not pre-scheduled, call to find out if there are any cancellations. Complete by the end of October if possible.

❑ Start working on applications and recommendations in early October, especially the essays.

❑ Apply very early to large state schools with limited housing.

❑ Decide by October (at the latest) if you'll apply for Early Action or Early Decision.

❑ Take SAT's or ACT's for the second (or third) time and Achievement Tests in November or, if necessary, December. (SAT's and Achievements must be taken on different days.)

❑ By December, at the latest, complete applications. Begin with those due first.

❑ If you are applying for financial aid, obtain copies of financial aid forms in December.

❑ As soon as possible after January 1, file your financial aid forms.

12th Grade / Spring Semester

❑ Keep up your grades and activities. Final grades usually go to colleges.

❑ By February, complete late applications.

❏ Continue visits and interviews, if necessary.

❏ When fall semester grades are complete, check with your guidance counselor to be sure that they are sent to all of your colleges along with additional supporting information (honors, prizes, late test scores, etc.).

❏ Make your final college choice by the required notification date.

❏ Inform (in writing) all of the colleges to which you've applied of your decision.

❏ Take senior year Advanced Placement (AP) exams.

Chapter X:

Financing College Costs

Financing College Costs

General Tips

❑ Think of financing college as an investment in your future.

❑ Start your financing plan as early as possible. Plan ahead and anticipate annual increases. Be realistic.

 You and/or your family have primary responsibility for financing your college education, not the government.

❑ Financial aid includes gifts (grants and scholarships which do not require repayment) and self-help (loans which must be repaid, and paying jobs). Aid may come from the federal or state government, from the college, or from other sources.

❑ Federal and state financial aid and tax laws and regulations change frequently. Be sure your information is up-to-date and accurate. Consider using *Update Service*.

❑ Consult a tax expert before making any personal or family financial decisions that might affect your eligibility for financial aid.

❑ Whether or not you're applying for financial aid, you should know what the realistic costs are going to be. Ask the colleges directly or consult *The College Cost Book* or *ACT's College Planning/Search Book.*

Don't automatically rule out any college because of costs. You may find a way to finance it. In fact, expensive private colleges may be able to offer more aid than less expensive colleges.

❑   Costs include tuition, mandatory fees, books and supplies, room and board, transportation, insurance, and personal expenses.

❑   An expensive college is not necessarily better.

❑   To help meet costs, consider:

- military service programs for men and women: military academies, ROTC. For more information, ask your guidance counselor, your college financial aid office, your local armed forces recruitment centers, or consult *How the Military Will Help You Pay for College.* Also, *Peterson's Guide to Four-Year Colleges* has a section on "The Army ROTC Program."

- taking tests to get credit for "out-of-school" learning.
  ☛ For more information: *The College Board Guide to CLEP Examinations; ACT PEP; Educational Testing Service (DANTES).*

- Co-op programs, available at over 1,000 public and private colleges and universities, where students work at jobs that are related to their studies. (Student earnings average about $7,000 per year.)
  ☛ For more information, consult The National Commission for Cooperative Education; The Cooperative Education Research Center; *Earn and Learn: Cooperative Education Opportunities Offered by the Federal Government.*

- working part-time and summers in an on- or off-campus, non-work-study job. Don't plan to work more than 15 hours/week while going to school full-time.

- offering a paid service, such as word processing or room cleaning

- getting college credits through correspondence courses.
  ☛ For more information: *Peterson's The Independent Study Catalog*; The National Home Study Council's *Directory of Accredited Home Study Schools.*

❑ Ask the college admissions office about ways of reducing your costs by shortening your college stay:

    ✓ credit for college courses taken in high school
    ✓ credit for Advanced Placement (AP) or Honor courses
    ✓ credit for work experiences

❑ Look into

- living at home and commuting to a community college for the first two years before transferring for the third and fourth years.

- "Three-Two Programs" which offer three years of undergraduate study plus two years of graduate study for a dual degree.

- accelerated degree programs in which you earn a bachelor's degree in three years.

- external degree programs in which credit may be earned in off-campus, non-traditional ways.
☛ For more information: *Bear's Guide to Earning Non-Traditional Degrees.*

❑ To qualify for the National Merit Scholarship and the National Achievement Scholarship Program for Outstanding Negro Students, you must take the PSAT in 11th grade. Criteria for scholarships vary by state.

❑ Veterans' groups, employers, unions, religious groups, and civic groups have financial aid programs. Consult reference materials in your local library and the Chamber of Commerce, or consult *Don't Miss Out.*

❑ If you've had military service, check the Veterans Educational Assistance Program, The GI Bill, other veterans' benefits, and state benefits.

❑ Various kinds of financial help are available if you're an athlete, a minority student, a woman, a handicapped student, or if you have interest in particular career fields.
☛ For more information, see *Don't Miss Out*; *The Black Student's Guide to Scholarships.*

❏ Ask your guidance counselor as soon as possible about non-government, private scholarships or grants for which you may be eligible.

❏ If you're a good student (at least a B average and 900+ SAT scores), investigate federal, state, or college no-need scholarships.
☛ For more information, *A's and B's of Academic Scholarships* and *Don't Miss Out.*

❏ If you're in the top 10% of your class and have financial need, you can apply in your senior year of high school for a Junior Fellowship. You would work in a federal agency during all college breaks and earn up to $10,000 in four years.
☛ For more information, see *Earn and Learn.*

❏ If a parent is employed by a college or university, you may be eligible for reduced tuition at that college or other colleges.

❏ If you are considering an out-of-state, public college, ask the Admissions Office about state residency requirements. You may be able to establish residency and then pay in-state costs.

❏ Residency requirements for in-state tuitions are established by state legislatures and vary from state to state.

❏ Each state has grant, scholarship, and loan programs for students who attend public colleges. Some states have programs for students who attend in-state private colleges. Many states have college financing plans for state residents. These include prepayment plans with tuition guarantee, tax-exempt savings accounts and bonds, and installment plan tuition certificates. Check with your state higher education agency. Call (800) 333-INFO for the address and phone number.
☛ For more information about state programs, consult *Don't Miss Out.*

❏ Some states and regions of the country have state-run programs which allow you to pay in-state or discounted prices at out-of-state colleges in the region. Check with your state higher education agency. Call (800) 333-INFO for the address and phone number.

❏   A few states have need-based grant programs for part-time students.

❏   Many colleges have special financing plans, such as low interest loans, tuition prepayment, and installment plans. Some offer reduced tuition for certain students or for attending classes at certain times. Investigate these possibilities.

❏   Several commercial organizations have tuition payment services. Consult the financial aid office or *Don't Miss Out.*

❏   If you are not eligible for financial aid but need a personal loan, check with the college financial aid office, your state agency, local banks, and investment companies. You may find a way to borrow at less than the going rate with acceptable repayment terms. Consider a PLUS loan (to qualify you must complete a financial aid form). For suggestions of private loan services, consult *Don't Miss Out.*

❏   Free computerized scholarship search services may be available in your high school guidance office. An electronic scholarship search service is available for about $13 from *Need a Lift?* Relatively costly ($40 or more) computerized financial aid search services are also available. The information they give may or may not be helpful. Be wary. They do not give you money. Several such services are listed in *Bear's Guide to Earning Non-Traditional College Degrees.*

❏   If you're confused and don't know where to begin with your financing plans, send for a free copy of Octameron's *We Can Help You.* Then consider using the services that are available for fees. For specific questions, you might want to use Octameron's financial aid phone consultation, available Tuesdays from 10 A.M. - 5 P.M. (Eastern time): (703) 823-1882. There is a $20 charge.

❏   Videos are available from the College Board on how to fill out financial aid forms and how to pay for college. Ask your guidance counselor.

❏   Free financial aid advice is available if you're the first in your low-income family to think about college. Consult the Educational Opportunity Center.

Applying for Financial Aid

❏ Financial aid is offered by each college. Your application for financial aid is separate from your application for admission. The financial aid office will tell you which forms you'll need.

❏ Applying for financial aid should not affect your chances for admission. College policies vary. Most colleges have "need-blind" admissions. Some, but relatively few, guarantee to meet the "demonstrated" financial needs of those they accept. Others try to meet the need, but there's no guarantee.

❏ It's a good idea to apply for federal financial aid even though you may be turned down. To qualify for many other types of aid, including federally guaranteed loans, you must go through this process.

❏ To qualify for most federal aid, you need to have a high school diploma, a GED, or the ability to benefit; be at least a half-time student; attend an accredited college; have financial need; be a U.S. citizen or eligible non-citizen.

 If you are male and 18 or older, you must be registered for selective service to be eligible for federal financial aid.

❏ Federal aid programs provide the majority of all financial aid. These are:

- **Pell Grants —**
  need-based; no repayment; direct to students
- **Supplemental Educational Opportunity Grants (SEOG) —**
  need-based; no repayment; priority for Pell Grant recipients; dispensed by colleges
- **Stafford Loans (formerly Guaranteed Student Loans) —**
  low-interest loans by lenders (banks, credit unions) to students; need-based; repayment required
- **Perkins Loans —**
  low-interest loans dispensed by colleges; need-based; repayment required

- **Parent Loans to Undergraduate Students (PLUS)** and
- **Supplemental Loans For Students (SLS)** —
   loans by lenders to parents or
   students; not need-based; repayment required
- **College Work Study (CWS)** —
   on or off-campus jobs for pay;
   administered by colleges; need-based

☞ For more information: Ask your guidance counselor
for a Federal Student Aid Fact Sheet or call the
Federal Student Aid Information Center (800) 333-INFO.

❏ To estimate if you are eligible for federal financial aid, get the College Board's *Meeting College Costs* or "Family Contribution Worksheet for Dependent Students" from your guidance counselor. Or follow the suggestions in *Don't Miss Out*.

❏ To get financial aid, you will need to complete an application form approved by the federal government. Contact the financial aid office of each college to which you're applying to get their application packets. The College Board's College Scholarship Service (CSS), Financial Aid Form (FAF), the ACT Program's Family Financial Statement (FFS), and the Application for Federal Student Aid are among the most commonly used. These forms should also be available in your guidance office. You may also be required to complete application forms for individual colleges and state programs.

❏ Some forms provide space for explaining any special financial circumstances. Use it if you want to explain anything unique or unusual about your situation.

❏ For divorced and step-families, financial aid rules vary as to who is responsible for meeting costs. Ask the college financial aid officer about this or ask your guidance counselor for The College Board's *Financial Aid Information for Students and Parents.*

❏ Follow directions exactly. Be absolutely accurate. If you receive aid based on incorrect information, you'll have to pay back the aid you should not have received. Errors may cause delays. Obtain help from your guidance office or a local college financial aid office if you are unsure. Make copies of the forms before you send the originals. Meet deadlines.

Be honest. It's a federal offense to lie on a financial aid form. You may be subject to a prison sentence, a $10,000 fine, or both.

❑ There are strict federal rules about declaring yourself an "independent student" (not financially dependent on your parents) for the purposes of qualifying for financial aid. If you do this, be sure you understand the rules.
☞ For more information: Call the Federal Student Aid Information Center (800) 333-INFO.

❑ The FAF form is sent to the College Board College Scholarship Service (CSS) or the FFS form is sent to the American College Testing Service (ACTS) for need analysis. The need analysis is then sent to the colleges you indicate. You will pay fees for this service.

❑ Your need is determined by a complex formula which examines your family's previous year's income, assets, and expenses to determine what you and your family can reasonably pay.

❑ Send your financial aid form as soon as possible after January 1, using information from the previous year's tax return. Allow 2 - 4 weeks for your form to be processed. If waiting for completion of the previous year's tax returns would result in missing college financial aid application deadlines, use reasonable estimates. You may be asked to send a signed copy of an income tax return later for verification. Some aid is awarded on a first-come, first-served basis, so don't delay.

❑ If there are major changes in your situation after you've sent the form, contact the college financial aid office.

❑ If any faculty members, coaches, or prominent alumni are anxious for you to attend the college you choose, ask them to speak to the financial aid office.

❑ You'll be sent an acknowledgment of the need analysis and a set of student aid reports. Check these reports (S.A.R.'s) carefully and correct if inaccurate.

❏ The college's definition of your need may differ considerably from yours. Your need is your college costs, as determined by the college, minus what you and your family can pay, as determined by your need analysis.

❏ If you are awarded financial aid, it generally comes as a package which may include:

- grants and/or scholarship from the college, the state, or the federal government (grants are usually need-based; scholarships may be based on need or merit — special academic, athletic, or artistic talent).

- work-study jobs (about 10-15 hours per week). These are a part of financial aid and are federally subsidized.

- low-interest, federally guaranteed loans

❏ If you receive financial aid, you will be expected to contribute a minimum of $700 from your summer or other earnings.

❏ When you receive your financial award offers, consider the debt on your loans and the repayment schedule. Are these acceptable to you? Remember, failure to repay loans may result in serious consequences. It's best to have a relatively high percentage of grants/scholarships and a low percentage of loans. Be aware that some types of aid might not be renewable.

❏ You must accept an award offer by the deadline or it may be cancelled. You can sometimes get a short extension.

❏ You may reject any part of the financial aid package that doesn't suit you.

❏ If your financial aid package doesn't offer as much as you need, call the financial aid office to see if they can give you more. If you've been offered more elsewhere, tell them this.

❏ All financial aid offices operate under strict government and college rules and have limited funds. Some colleges have per-student limits on aid.

- Generally, the more desirable you are as an applicant, the better your chances of receiving aid based on merit. If you're very desirable, you may be offered a no-need award as an enticement.

- Private colleges generally have more flexibility in offering aid than public colleges.

- All information you send to financial aid offices is confidential.

- Financial aid is awarded one year at a time and may include "one-time" offers. To be awarded aid again, you must meet the college's satisfactory progress standards. You'll need to reapply annually. The deadlines may differ and the package may change.

- If you've not been awarded aid in your freshman year, chances of getting it later are slim, unless your financial situation has changed considerably, the number of family members attending college at least half-time increases, or you transfer to another college.

- Financial aid awards do not transfer from one college to another. If you transfer during the academic year, contact the financial aid office at your new college for information on what to do to receive aid.

In addition to the references previously mentioned, you may wish to consult the following:

- *College Check Mate: Innovative Tuition Plans That Make You a Winner*

- *College Loans from Uncle Sam: The Borrower's Guide That Explains It All*

- *College Grants from Uncle Sam: Am I Eligible and For How Much?*

- *Federal Educational and Scholarship Funding Guide*

- *Financial Aid Fin-Ancer: Expert Answers to College Financing Questions*

- *Financial Aid Officers: What They Do To You and For You*

- *Need a Lift? To Educational Opportunities, Careers, Loans, Scholarships, Employment*

- *Paying for Your Education: A Guide for Adult Learners*

- *Peterson's College Money Handbook*

- *75 Scholarships Every Black High School Student Should Know About*

- *Winning Money for College: The High School Student's Guide to Scholarship Contests.*

Chapter XI:

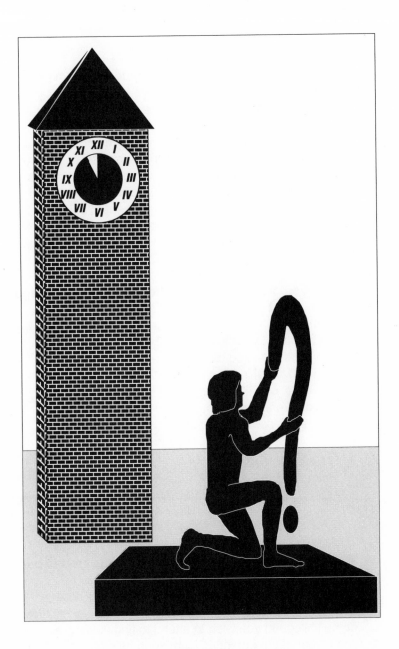

What If?

What If?

?   **What if you didn't complete high school but now want to attend college?**
Contact the guidance office of the last high school you attended to obtain a copy of your transcript. Ask a guidance counselor about preparing for and possibly taking or retaking some of the standardized tests. Consult your local high school and your local community college about ways of taking courses and getting credits toward your high school diploma. If you are over 25, some colleges may waive the high school diploma requirement. Follow procedures for selecting and applying to colleges.

?   **What if you completed high school a year or more ago and now want to attend college?**
Contact the high school from which you graduated to obtain a copy of your transcript. Consider taking or retaking standardized tests. Present what you've done since high school in the most positive way possible on your applications. If you can't attend college full time, try day or evening part-time attendance, weekend college, adult education classes for credit, business training classes, or correspondence courses.

☛ For more information, see *The College Board Guide to CLEP Examinations; ACT PEP; Educational Testing Service (DANTES); Bear's Guide to Earning Non-Traditional College Degrees; Going to College While Working: Strategies for Success.*

?   **What if you have an assortment of college credits but now want to get your degree?**
Same as above. Also, get a transcript from the college or colleges you attended. Consult the Admissions Office of the college(s) you wish to attend to find out degree completion requirements. If you need help consolidating your academic records and preparing your transcript, Regents Credit Bank provides such a service.

? **What if a traditional college where you would attend classes is not for you, but you need or want a college degree?**
Consult *Bear's Guide to Earning Non-Traditional College Degrees* for information about earning credits and degrees from non-classroom experiences, equivalency examinations, correspondence courses, and learning contracts. Be sure in advance that the non-traditional credits or degree will meet your needs. Most non-traditional college programs have relatively easy admissions requirements and low costs. For personal help with a non-traditional education plan, contact Degree Consulting Services.

? **What if you're college-bound but want some time off after high school?**
Complete high school courses and standardized testing as if you were going directly to college. Get letters of recommendation for your file. You can apply to colleges that offer **deferred admission** and then, once accepted, request a postponement of your college entrance. Or you can apply later, during your time off. In either case, it's good to use some of your time off for learning (courses, creative work, independent projects), especially if you intend to apply to selective colleges. You might want to contact the American Institute for Foreign Study (AIFS), the International Christian Youth Exchange, the Open Door Student Exchange, Dynamy, or the Peace Corps.

? **What if you want to go to college but think you would benefit from an additional year in high school?**
Several independent schools accept post-graduate (PG) students for one year. Costs range from $5,000 to $12,000 and entrance is competitive. Apply during fall semester of your 12th grade.
☞ For more information, see *Boarding Schools: Special Programs.*

? **What if you want to enter college in the middle of the year?**
Some colleges permit mid-year admissions, but this option isn't always listed in the college guidebooks. Call the college Admissions Offices to inquire about policies and procedures.

? **What if you're in 11th grade but you think you have a strong enough high school record and enough maturity to enter college without completing 12th grade?**
Many colleges offer Early Entrance. Start the process early, in the fall of 11th grade for admission the following fall. If you start later, you might try for mid-year admission the following year. Be prepared to complete your 12th grade if you are not accepted. Look for local opportunities to take college level courses for credit.

? **What if you're accepted at one or more of the colleges to which you apply but can't decide which one to attend?**
If possible, visit and stay overnight, even if you've done this before. Consider all the pros and cons and discuss them with others. If it still isn't clear, any one of your choices will probably be fine.

? **What if you're on the waiting list of the college you really want to attend, but are accepted at one or more of the colleges you wouldn't mind attending?**
Don't count on the waiting list. Send a deposit to hold a place at one of the colleges at which you've been accepted. If you're accepted later at your wait-list college, notify the other college of your change of plans.

? **What if you're not accepted anywhere but are on at least one waiting list?**
Don't count on the waiting list. Start making some alternate plans, just in case.

? **What if you're not accepted or on the waiting list *anywhere* ?**
Remember, your *application* was turned down, not you personally. Analyze what you could have done better. Were you realistic in your choices? Did you work hard on your

applications? Then try the following:

◆ Try to attend one of your chosen colleges part-time as a non-matriculated student. If you do well, you may be accepted later.

◆ Get a list of colleges that still have openings from the Independent Educational Counselors Association or from your state higher education agency. Call (800) 333-INFO for address and phone number.

◆ Even in August, many colleges with rolling admissions still have openings for fall. Make a list of colleges you wouldn't mind attending. Telephone the admissions offices to see if they still have openings and housing. Then proceed with applications.

◆ Attend your local community college, earn good grades, and plan to transfer.

◆ Plan to do something interesting and worthwhile during your "year off" and apply again. It's OK to reapply to colleges that denied you admission, especially if you present a stronger application.

? **What if you want or need to transfer to another college?** Only certain types of credits and associate degrees transfer. Generally, credits comparable to those offered by the transfer college are accepted. Credits from technical and correspondence courses and CLEP examinations may not be accepted.

You might need to take some courses that you didn't take in high school.

Transfers are usually made after two years, but they may be possible after one year or even one semester.

Consult the guidance office of your present college for information and, if available, a transfer manual. Get a Transfer Guide from the college(s) you want to attend.

Your college grades, activities, and recommendations will be more important than those from your high school, but you might consider re-taking standardized tests.

Be sure that at least one college professor knows you well enough to write you a favorable recommendation.

You should have at least a 2.0 Grade Point Average. (Some colleges require 2.5 or 3.0 GPA for transfers.)

You also should have a good reason for transferring, such as going from a two-year college to a four-year college, or because your chosen major is unavailable.

You might want to re-apply to colleges that previously denied you admission if you now have a strong college record.

Treat your transfer application just as seriously as an original application.

It may be easier to get into a four-year state college from a community college in that state than into a private college.

When selecting colleges to which you might transfer, check the number of transfers accepted. It can be difficult to be a transfer student at a college that accepts very few, even if you do get in.

You may not be notified about admission until late summer. Be sure you have back-up plans.

? **What if you and your parents disagree about your college choices?**
Keep them informed about what you're thinking. Have good, defensible reasons for your choices. Explain calmly and persuasively. Listen to their concerns and points of view. Be realistic. Negotiate. In most cases, you can reach an agreement. If you're still having trouble, consider using a consultant or other outsider to be a mediator. Suggest that they read *The College Guide for Parents*. The ultimate choice should be yours.

? What if you have a physical handicap or a learning disability and will need special conditions or support?

Talk freely to an admissions officer about your needs. If you have a learning disability, it's good to talk to an admissions officer who is a learning specialist. Most colleges can accommodate students with physical handicaps. Many have special support services for LD students. Consider using Lovejoy's personal counseling service for LD Students.

☛ For further information: *Peterson's Guide to Colleges with Programs for Learning-Disabled Students; Information for Students with Special Needs; Campus Opportunities for the Learning-Disabled Student;* Lovejoy's *College Guide for the Learning Disabled; Colleges That Enable: A Guide to Support Services Offered to Physically Disabled Students on 40 U.S. Campuses.*

? What if you're a foreign-born or American student overseas who wishes to study at a college in the United States?

If English is not your first language, you will probably take the TOEFL for college admission. Find out if the colleges you are considering offer "English as a Second Language" programs during the academic year. Contact the College Board's Office of International Education for help through the Foreign Student Information Clearinghouse and/or through written guides.

☛ For more information: *Entering Higher Education in the United States: A Guide for Students from Other Countries.*

? What if you're a black student and can't decide whether to go to a predominantly black college or a predominantly white college?

Get information about and visit both types. Talk to other black students about their college experiences. Ask your guidance counselor about special college days, summer programs, and financial aid for minority students. *The Black Student 's Guide to Colleges* or *I Am Somebody* might be helpful.

? What if you're a Hispanic student and need educational guidance not provided by your high school?

Consult ASPIRA Association, Inc., which provides leadership development and educational services for Latino college-bound students.

? **What if you're a student from a low-income family that has no experience with college applications or attendance?**
Contact the Educational Opportunity Center for free academic and financial aid advice.

? **What if you're a woman and can't decide whether to go to woman's college or a co-ed college?**
Get information about and visit both types. Talk to other women about their college experiences.
☛ For more information: *Get Smart: A Woman's Guide to Equality on Campus; Women's College Coalition; Happier By Degrees.*

? **What if you're a woman who's considering returning to school?**
Read *Smart Choices*, which gives insight, encouragement, and practical advice.

? **What if you want to attend a religious or Bible college and want to be sure that it's legitimately accredited?**
Contact the American Association of Bible Colleges for a list of accredited colleges.

? **What if you're a senior citizen?**
Many colleges will be happy to have you as a student, full- or part-time. You may be eligible for financial aid or reduced tuition. Exceptions to formal admissions requirements may be possible. Check with the colleges.

☛ For more information: *Learning Opportunities for Older Persons; Directory of Centers for Older Learners.*

Chapter XII:

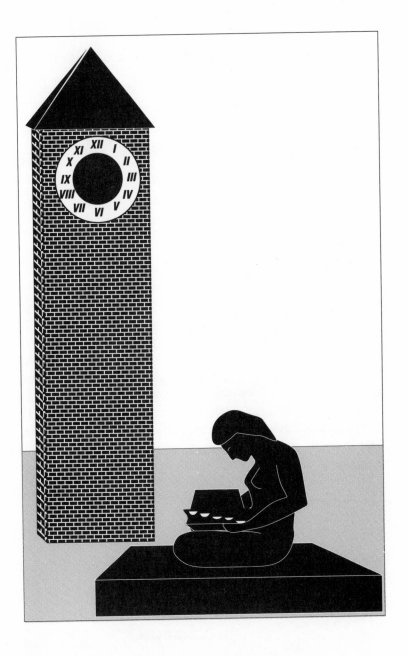

Samples and Resources

Samples

Sample letter requesting information from a college:

(Date)

(Name of Admissions Director)
(Title)
(College Name)
(College Address)

Dear Mr. or Ms. (Name of Director):

I am a high school junior, and I plan to enter college in the fall of (year). Please send me information about (name of college). Specifically, I would like a view book, a catalog, an application form, financial aid information, a profile of the most recent freshman class, and any additional information you can provide on (major/program/or service). Please send these to:

(your name)
(your address)

Thank you for your help. I look forward to hearing from you soon.

Sincerely,
(your name)

Sample thank you letter to interviewer:

(Date)

(Name of interviewer)
(Title of interviewer)
(Address of interviewer)

Dear (Name of interviewer):

Thank you very much for talking with me on (date of interview). I was pleased to have the opportunity to learn more about (name of college or a topic discussed). I am now convinced that I would like to be a student at (name of college). I plan to submit my application by (date) and hope that I will be accepted.

Sincerely,
(your name)

Here are some essay questions you might find on your applications:

✎ Tell us something about yourself that we might not learn from the rest of your application.

✎ Write a brief essay that in some way describes who you are.

✎ Which adjective would best describe you by those who know you best?

✎ Describe a significant experience or achievement that has special meaning for you.

✎ What is the most meaningful (joyful, frightening) experience you've ever had?

✎ What is the best piece of advice you've ever received?

✎ If you were to spend three months alone and were allowed to have only three non-essential items, what would they be? Why would you choose them?

✎ What responsibility have you had for others, and how has it affected your personal growth?

✎ Whom do you admire most? Why?

✎ If you could travel through time and interview any historical figure, who would you choose, what would you ask, and why?

✎ If you could spend a day with one famous person, who would that be and why?

✎ If you were able to change one thing about your community or country, what would you change? Why?

✎ Discuss some issue of personal, local, national, or international concern and its importance to you.

✎ Discuss a piece of art or literature. Why has it been meaningful to you? What have you learned from it?

✎ Make up a question, state it clearly, and answer it.

Here are some questions you might be asked during your interview with an admissions officer:

- Why do you want to go to college?

- Why do you think you'd like to attend this college?

- What do you want to do in the future?

- What do you hope to major in? Why?

- Tell me about yourself.

- What are your greatest strengths? Greatest weaknesses?

- Do you consider yourself an expert in anything?

- What have you liked most about your high school?

- What have you liked least about your high school?

- Do you think that your grades and test scores give a true picture of the kind of work you can do?

- What do you like to do in your spare time?

- What book or movie have you particularly enjoyed lately?

- What do you think is the most serious problem in the world today?

- If you could have three wishes come true, what would you wish?

- Do you have any relatives who've attended this college?

- What other colleges are you considering?

- What questions would you like to ask about this college?

Here are some things you might want to learn from college publications or during campus visits, but probably not during your admissions interview:

● What was last year's freshman attrition rate? What percent flunked out? What percent were asked to leave?

● What was the percent of faculty turnover in the last five years? What is the educational background of the faculty? What is their teaching experience?

● What is the background of the college president? Is he/she well-liked?

● Who are the trustees and how supportive are they?

● Does the college have an endowment? If so, how much has it grown in the last five years?

● What percent of the alumni contributed to the college last year? What have been the recent trends in alumni donations? What else do alumni do for the college?

● How well does the college get along with the community? What opportunities are there for the students to interact with the community?

● How do students get around on campus and travel off campus?

● How and to what extent are computers used in this college?

● What do you or don't you need to bring for your dorm room?

● What kind of social life predominates?

● How's the food?

● What types of student activism, if any, are common on campus? What is the college response to disruptive students?

● To what extent are there problems with burglaries, rape, suicide, substance abuse, and discrimination? What is the college doing about these?

Sample Essays

The essays that follow were chosen by college admissions officers to be included in *Essays That Worked*, a book of 50 outstanding application essays. Aside from being well-written, each essay gives the reader a glimpse at the *individual* applicant, a chance to see the person behind all the grades and test scores. We hope these essays will show you that there's a wide variety of essays that "work," and we hope they will inspire you as you begin to write.

Melinda Menzer

Sometimes I sit in my room and try to move things. I stare as hard as I can at, say, a tissue box and think, "MOVE!" Crinkling up my forehead, scrunching up my eyes, I will with all might that the tissue box will levitate. So far, nothing has ever moved. But I am still hoping to develop extra-sensory powers.

I guess what I fear most is being ordinary. Well, let me qualify that. I fear nuclear holocaust, robbers under the bed, big, furry tarantulas, and the theft of my dear teddy bear, Phoebe, just as much or more. But I don't want to be ordinary. Ordinary is boring; ordinary is pointless; ordinary is so very...ordinary. Anyone can be ordinary. But I don't want to be just anyone.

Reading *Crime and Punishment* made me think about being ordinary. Raskolnikov, the main character, wants to prove that he is extraordinary, that he is a super-man. To do this, he kills a woman pawnbroker. Now, I don't need to kill anybody; I am a tad more laid back than Raskolnikov. But I, too, want to do something. I have a predilection towards living in a garret, eating ketchup soup and Saltines, writing the The Great American Novel. Or, like Larry Darrell in *The Razor's Edge*, I could travel the world in search of truth, doing good "for the love of a God he doesn't believe in." I want to sacrifice for a worthy cause; I want to change the world; I want to make the difference.

Now, they tell me I'm a pretty smart cookie. I have the credentials: good SAT scores, National Merit Semifinalist, four AP classes. As cookies go, I'm near the top of the jar. But am I a boring, bland, sugar cookie or an ordinary, carbon copy, buy-at-the-supermarket cookie? Or am I a super-duper, slightly eccentric, rough but delicious, homemade, one-of-a-kind oatmeal-raisin cookie? I refuse to be just another ordinary cookie in the crowd. Eventually I'll win the Nobel Prize for Literature, or I'll discover the nature of genetic processes. Perhaps tomorrow will be the day I make the tissue box move. ■

Jennifer Dodge

It is tempting to describe myself to you in terms of grades, more lists of extra-curricular activities, to expound on my love of reading, to, in fact, try to wow you with my attributes. But I'm uncomfortable with that, and you still wouldn't know any more about me as a person. I'm going to try to give you some insight into me by relating one experience and its ramifications.

My friends and I have a special word to perfectly describe an "ah hah experience". The word is Whomp! (You pronounce the wh as if you saying what.) We use this word to describe what happens when something really hits you hard. For example: "I left my Accounting project at home, and, Whomp!, Mrs. Winslow gave me *six* extra assignments as a consequence!" Or, "I couldn't believe he took her out. Whomp! It's really over between us."

Okay. I hope you now have an idea of the significance of the word. With that as background I can tell you about the biggest Whomp! of my life. It happened early in October, 1984, during my junior year. I was with a group of friends at a cabin in the hills of Eastern Iowa. While standing on a balcony approximately thirty-five feet above the rocky terrain, the supports under the balcony gave way. Luckily for me, the ground broke my fall; unluckily, my leg did the same. One minute I was a healthy, mobile sixteen year old and, Whomp!, the next I had a leg in about fourteen different pieces, with some of those pieces protruding through a gaping wound.

My memories of the next few days are rather hazy. I can remember my mother's worried face hovering over me from time to time. I remember being told that I'd been through surgery and that they'd (the wondrous orthopedists) packed the bones together and fastened them at each end with pins. "Cool. You'll beep the airport metal detectors, Jen," my brother told me. Well, I'd also have sore armpits (crutches became by best friend and worst brother), and a cast up to my hip for six months. It seemed like an eternity.

Physical pain was the least of my worries. Whomp! People stared at me now. I couldn't take a shower. I couldn't go jogging. I couldn't stand for very long. I couldn't be on the track team. I couldn't get down to the newspaper room at school. I could watch TV—small compensation. I felt totally helpless and very frustrated at times. I needed help getting dressed, and getting to class, and getting into the car...

Wait a minute, this cast is only going to be on for six more months. Whomp! Some people are like this for their entire life. Some people have much worse problems that they must deal with every day of their existence with no light at the end of a six-month tunnel.

This really got me thinking. What would it be like to be physically handicapped? Dependent your whole life? These insights made me want to get involved. They made me want to do something to make a difference.

Now it's my senior year. Handicapped students (trainably mentally retarded kids, some with physical handicaps too) have been brought to Westside for their Special Education classes. I went to see the Department Head of Special Education. Together we devised a club called Peer Advocates which is like a buddy system between the regular education and special education kids. We have tried to pair the non-handicapped with the handicapped students according to interests and personalities. They are required to spend at least four hours a month with their match. We are also planning several group field trips to places like the zoo and bowling.

Organizing this group has been one of the most meaningful things I've ever done. Now kids of two totally different lifestyles are going out to lunch together and learning things about each other that they could never have learned from reading a book or studying handicaps. We are all learning compassion and tolerance and understanding. As for myself, I feel as though I'm doing something extremely worthwhile. For example, one morning, after a breakfast meeting of the group, a boy with Downs Syndrome named David walked up to me with a huge smile and gave me a great bear hug. He told me that he was so happy to have a special friend at Westside and thanked me. That was all I needed to know that the idea had been a good one. ∎

Maeve O'Connor

Last Thursday was my father's birthday. I was standing on the sideline at my soccer game, shivering in the cold October drizzle, when suddenly I remembered. He would have been 53.

When I got home that day, Mom was in her room, sorting through some of my father's old sketch books. She had remembered too. I told her I thought we should spend the evening doing something Dad would have liked to do, and she smiled and said that was a wonderful idea. We selected a symphony by Beethoven from the stacks of records in the music room, and then the five of us gathered close around the small kitchen table for dinner. We ate by candlelight, laughing as we remembered.

No one had made a birthday cake, so when we had finished we went to Brigham's for ice cream. My father had loved to take us there on special occasions. I would have liked a dish of mocha almond, but I ordered chocolate chip with jimmies, just like I used to every time Dad took us to Brigham's when I was small.

It's cold out today, and I'm wearing my father's Irish sweater. He used to wear this sweater all the time on winter weekends. It has big holes in the shoulders that he never bothered to sew, but it's thick and warm, and our old house is drafty. In the past year or so, one of the holes has stretched so far that I'm afraid the entire sleeve will come off, but I don't want to mend it. I love the holes. ∎

David Bolognia

My Nightly Ritual
(Heretofore Kept Secret)

The best thing to eat day or night, winter or summer, anywhere in the world, at anytime, inside, outside, or upside down, alone, or with a friend, is an Oreo cookie. I do not refer to any Oreo cookie, but to the singularly succulent sustenance which retains its number one position on the weekly top-forty goody list, month after month. Of course, I refer to the extremely palatable Doublestuff. Being a self-taught connoisseur of this craft, I will share my experiences on exactly how to eat these desirous, delectable delights.

First and foremost, I make extra sure Mom has them on her shopping list weekly. Oreos without milk is like Laurel without Hardy, so obviously, the second requirement is milk; it must be cold and it must be fresh. The glass in which to pour the milk must be short and fat, not tall and thin, for dunking purposes, of course. If the preliminary steps have been completed and my perspicacious dog has not discovered my intentions yet, it only means more for me. (There are ways to trick even the wisest of dogs, but let us not digress here.)

Once all the materials are gathered, I recline in a dimly lit room and pig out. Taking one at a time so as to relish every bite makes for a most memorable event. I never eat the whole cookie right away because much can be told about a person by the way he eats his Doublestuffs, and this method designates a boring personality.

First, I turn the chocolate cookie part in a clockwise direction and pull lightly, never pulling too hard so as to break it. I dunk half the chocolate piece in the milk, eat it, and toss the remaining half to appease the dog drooling on my leg. At this point, depending on the mood and company, there are different methods to follow. If time is short, I dunk the rest of the cookie, quickly swirling it so as to soften it and plop the whole piece in my mouth. If I feel it's weakening, the process is even quicker, because there is nothing worse than slugged milk. It is imperative to remember that a cookie in the mouth is worth two in the glass.

The classic style in Nabisco is the "bucky-beaver bite." It is done by scraping the front teeth down across the white cream paying particular attention to what is done so as not to bump the nose on the hard cookie. Once it is one my tongue, I fling my head back, swallowing it delicately. Of course, this method leaves another plain chocolate cookie, which the dog will gladly devour.

However, my all time favorite method of eating an Oreo is to build a bigger cookie; we have the technology. For this more complicated process, a butterknife is a necessity. The disassembling process is repeated. Now both chocolate sections must be removed from subsequent cookies. Here the butterknife comes in handy. This must be done gently so as not to break the cookie. The cream fillings are to be carefully stacked one on top of the other until guilt sets in or it no longer fits in the mouth. There is an option of eating the extra chocolates or gaining a life long friend in the now salivating dog. After admiring my creation, I "dunk-n-devour."

Lastly, every drop of milk is consumed while searching for drowning bits and pieces. Now I rinse the glass and take a follow-up swig of clean, fresh milk.

Following these easy instructions, even the most simple-minded person can become a creditable cookie consumer. Using any of these methods, I encourage everyone to partake in this epicurean delight. I am positive if all the men, women, and children of this world were to join in the sublime ritual of this art, we would have the happiest planet in the Milky Way. And now I feel this overwhelming urge to retire to the kitchen for more research. ∎

Resource List

AP Program
The College Board
45 Columbus Ave.
New York, NY 10023
(212) 713-8000

AP Services
PO Box 6671
Princeton, NJ 08541
(609) 921-9000

ACT National Office
ACT PEP
ACT's Educational Opportunity Service
ACT Publications
PO Box 168
Iowa City, IA 52243
(319) 337-1000

ACT DISCOVER Center
230 Schilling Circle
Hunt Valley, MD 21031
(301) 584-8000

Air Force ROTC
Headquarters
Maxwell AFB, AL 36112
(205) 293-5908

American Assoc. of Bible Colleges
PO Box 1523
Fayetteville, AR 72702
(501) 521-8164

American Institute for Foreign Study
102 Greenwich Ave.
Greenwich, CT 06830
(203) 869-9090

America's Best Colleges
U.S. News & World Report
2400 N St. NW
Washington, DC 20037
(202) 955-2000

Army ROTC
PO Box 1688
Ellicott City, MD 21043
(800) USA-ROTC

ASPIRA Association
1112 6th St. NW #304
Washington, DC 20036
(202) 835-3600

ATP Services for Handicapped Students
PO Box 6226
Princeton, NJ 08541
(609) 771-7600

Barron's Guide to the Most Prestigious Colleges
Barron's Profiles of American Colleges
Barron's Inc.
PO Box 8040
Hauppage, NY 11788
(800) 645-3476

Bear's Guide to Earning Non-Traditional
   College Degrees
Ten Speed Press
PO Box 7123
Berkeley, CA 94707
(800) 841-BOOK

The Black Student's Guide to Colleges
The Black Student's Guide to Scholarships
Beckham House Publishers
PO Box 177
Hampton, VA 23669
(804) 728-9303

Boarding Schools: Special Programs
National Assoc. of Independent Schools
18 Tremont St.
Boston, MA 01208
(617) 723-6900

The Center for Interim Programs
233 Mt. Lucas Rd.
Princeton, NJ 08540
(609) 924-1310

CLEP
PO Box 1824
Princeton, NJ 08541
(609) 771-7600

College Board Admissions Testing
   Program (ATP)
PO Box 6200
Princeton, NJ 08541
(609) 771-7600

College Board Office of International Education
1717 Massachusetts Ave. NW
Washington, DC 20036
(202) 332-7134

College Board publications:
10 SAT's
Campus Visits and College Interviews
College Board Achievement Tests
College Board Guide for Parents
College Board Guide to CLEP Examinations
College Board Guide to Going to College While
   Working
The College Cost Book
College Explorer (computer program)
The College Handbook
Entering Higher Education in the United States:
   A Guide for Students from Other Countries
Information for Students with Special Needs
Meeting College Costs

Paying for Your Education: A Guide for Adult
   Learners
Summer on Campus: College Experiences for
   High School Students
Taking the SAT (video)
Test-Sense/Test-Wise (software)
Your College Application
The College Board
PO Box 886
New York, NY 10101
(212) 713-8165

College Board videos:
College Choice, Student Choice
Completing the FAF
Paying for College
Taking the SAT
West Glen Film Library
1430 Broadway
New York, NY 10018
(212) 921-2800

Colleges That Enable: A Guide to Support
   Services Offered to Physically Disabled
   Students on 40 U.S. Campuses
Park Avenue Press
811 Grandview Rd.
Oil City, PA 16301
(814) 676-5777

Comparative Guide to American Colleges
HarperCollins
10 E. 53rd St.
New York, NY 10022
(800) 242-7737

DANTES Program
Educational Testing Service
Princeton, NJ 08541
(609) 921-9000

Degree Consulting Services
PO Box 3533
Santa Rosa, CA 95402
(707) 539-6466

Directory of Centers for Older Learners
Learning Opportunities for Older Persons
American Assoc. of Retired Persons (AARP)
1909 K St. NW
Washington, DC 20049
(202) 872-4700

Dynamy (supervised internships)
27 Sever St.
Worcester, MA 01609
(508) 755-2571

Education Opportunities Center
26 Franklin St.
Worcester, MA 01608
(508) 755-2592

*Essays That Worked: 50 Essays from
 Successful Applications to the Nation's
 Top Colleges*
Mustang Publishing
PO Box 3004
Memphis, TN 38173
(901) 521-1406

*Federal Educational and Scholarship Funding
 Guide*
Grayco Publishing
PO Box 1291
W. Warwick, RI 02893
(401) 821-2750

Federal Student Aid Information Center
(800) 333-INFO

Financial Aids for Higher Education
William C. Brown Publishing
2460 Kerper Blvd.
Dubuque, IA 52001
(800) 553-4920

The Fiske Guide to Colleges
Random House
201 E. 50th St.
New York, NY 10022
(800) 638-6460

*Get Smart: A Woman's Guide to Equality on
 Campus*
The Talman Co.
150 5th Ave.
New York, NY 10011
(800) 537-8894

The GIS Guide to Four-Year Colleges
Houghton Mifflin Co.
2 Park St.
Boston, MA 02108
(617) 725-5000

*The Gourman Report: A Rating of Undergradu-
 ate Programs*
Dearborn Trade
520 N. Dearborn St.
Chicago, IL 60610
(312) 836-0466

Gruber's Complete Preparation for the SAT
HarperCollins
10 E. 53rd St.
New York, NY 10022
(800) 242-7737

Guide to Accredited Camps
American Camping Assoc.
5000 State Rd. 67N
Martinsville, IN 46151
(317) 342-8456

*Happier By Degrees: The Complete Guide for
 Women Returning to College or Just
 Starting Out*
Ten Speed Press
PO Box 7123
Berkeley, CA 94707
(800) 841-BOOK

*How to Get an Ivy League Education at a State
 University*
Avon Books
1790 Broadway
New York, NY 10019
(800) 247-5470

Independent Educational Consultants Assoc.
PO Box 125
Forrestdale, MA 02644
(508) 477-2127

The Insider's Guide to the Colleges
St. Martin's Press
175 5th Ave.
New York, NY 10010
(800) 221-7945

International Christian Youth Exchange
134 W. 26th St.
New York, NY 10001
(212) 206-7307

Lovejoy's College Guide to Financial Aid
Simon & Schuster
1 Gulf & Western Plaza
New York, NY 10023
(212) 333-5800

Lovejoy Offices
   (personal counseling for LD students)
130 Maple Ave. #3A
Red Bank, NJ 07701
(201) 741-5640

National Assoc. of College Admissions
   Counselors
1800 Diagonal Rd. #430
Alexandria, VA 22314
(703) 836-2222

*NCAA Guide for the College-Bound Student
   Athlete*
National Collegiate Athletic Assoc.
6201 College Blvd.
Overland Park, KS 66211
(913) 384-3226

National Commission for Cooperative
   Education
PO Box 999
Boston, MA 02115
(617) 437-3778

National Home Study Council
   (directory of accredited home study schools)
1601 18th St. NW
Washington, DC 20009
(202) 234-5100

National Society for Internships and
   Experiential Education
3509 Haworth Dr. #207
Raleigh, NC 27609
(919) 787-3263

Navy/Marine Corps ROTC
4015 Wilson Blvd.
Arlington, VA 22203
(800) 327-NAVY

Need a Lift?
Emblem Sales
PO Box 1050
Indianapolis, IN 46206
(317) 635-8411

Octameron's College Selection Service
Octameron's Financial Aid Phone Consultation
Octameron publications:
The A's and B's of Academic Scholarships
Admit One! Your Guide to College Application
*Campus Opportunities for the Learning Dis-
   abled Student*

*College Check Mate: Innovative Tuition Plans
   That Make You a Winner*
College Grants from Uncle Sam
College Loans from Uncle Sam
*Don't Miss Out: The Ambitious Student's Guide
   to Financial Aid*
*Earn & Learn: Cooperative Education Opportu-
   nities Offered by the Federal Government*
*Financial Aid Fin-Ancer: Expert Answers to
   College Financing Questions*
*Financial Aid Officers: What They Do to You
   and for You*
Financial Aid Software
I Am Somebody
Update Service (follows changes in federal
   student aid regulations)
We Can Help You (personalized assistance)
*The Winning Edge: A Complete Guide to
   Intercollegiate Athletic Programs*
Octameron Associates
PO Box 3437
Alexandria, VA 22303
(703) 836-5480

Open Door Student Exchange
PO Box 71
Hempstead, NY 11551
(516) 486-7330

Peace Corps
1990 K St. NW
Washington, DC 20526
(800) 424-8580

Peterson's publications:
College Money Handbook
College Quest
College Video Library
Competitive Colleges
Guide to Four-Year Colleges
*Guide to Colleges with Learning-Disabled
   Students*
Guide to Two-Year Colleges
How the Military Will Help You Pay for College
The Independent Study Catalog
SAT Panic Plan
SAT Success
Smart Choices
Summer Opportunities for Kids and Teenagers
*Winning Money for College: The High School
   Student's Guide to Scholarship Contests*
Peterson's Guides
PO Box 2123
Princeton, NJ 08543
(800) EDU-DATA

The Princeton Review
   (standardized test preparation)
10 Columbus Circle #1260
New York, NY 10019
(800) 333-0369

Princeton Review's Cracking the System: The
   SAT
Random House
201 E. 50th St.
New York, NY 10022
(800) 638-6460

PSAT/NMSQT
PO Box 6720
Princeton, NJ 08541
(609) 921-9000

The Public Ivys
Viking Penguin
40 W. 23rd St.
New York, NY 10010
(212) 337-5200

Regents Credit Bank
Regents College
SUNY Cultural Education Center
Albany, NY 12230
(518) 473-8957

The Right College
A Taste of College: On-Campus Summer
   Programs for High School Students
Arco/Simon & Schuster
1 Gulf & Western Plaza
New York, NY 10023
(212) 333-5800

Stanley Kaplan Educational Centers
   (standardized test preparation)
131 W. 56th St.
New York, NY 10019
(800) KAP-TEST

Summer Jobs: Opportunities in the Federal
   Government
U.S. Office of Personnel Management
1900 E St. NW
Washington, DC 20413
(202) 275-7288

Summer Options for Teenagers
PO Box 254
Acton, MA 01720
(508) 263-8921

TOEFL/TSE
PO Box 6154
Princeton, NJ 08541
(609) 921-9000

Up Your SAT Score
New Chapter Press
391 Park Ave. S. #1122
New York, NY 10016
(212) 683-4090

Women's College Coalition
1101 17th St. NW #1001
Washington, DC 20036
(202) 466-5430

About the Authors

Lois Rochester is an independent school and college consultant. She is a graduate of Barnard College and has a Masters in Education from the University of Virginia. Before moving to Virginia, Lois was the Assistant Head of the Riverdale Country School in New York. She is married and the mother of two daughters, both of whom are college graduates.

Judy Mandell is a freelance writer, computer teacher, and director of development of a small, independent school. A graduate of Cornell, she has been chairman of Cornell University's Alumni Admissions Ambassador Network in central Virginia for 10 years. Judy is married and the mother of two sons and a daughter, two of whom are college graduates, while the third is in college.

More Great Books
from Mustang Publishing

Essays That Worked: 50 Essays from Successful Applications to the Nation's Top Colleges by Boykin Curry & Brian Kasbar. Applying to college? Dread the essay? This book can help. With 50 outstanding essays from schools like Yale, Duke, and Wesleyan—plus lots of helpful advice from admissions officers—this book will inspire any college applicant who needs help with the all-important essay. *"50 admissions essays, each one a winner"* — New York Times. **$8.95**

Also available in this series:
Essays That Worked—For Business Schools by Boykin Curry & Brian Kasbar. **$8.95**

Essays That Worked—For Law Schools by Boykin Curry. **$8.95**

Medical School Admissions: The Insider's Guide by John A. Zebala and Daniel B. Jones. Written by two students at Cornell Medical School, this book is the most complete, practical guide to the medical admissions process available. With information on the New Revised MCAT, unique study tips and application techniques, and 50 successful AMCAS essays, this book is essential for all would-be doctors. *"Applicants and their advisers will want this book"* — Booklist. **$10.95**

Europe for Free by Brian Butler. If you think a trip to Europe will be a long exercise in cashing traveler's checks, then this is the book for you! **Europe for Free** describes *thousands* of fun things to see and do all over Europe—and nothing costs one single lira, franc, or pfennig. *"A valuable resource"* — U.P.I. **$8.95**

Let's Blow thru Europe by Thomas Neenan & Greg Hancock. For the 14-cities-in-14-days traveler, this book is a must! Easily the funniest travel guide ever written, **Let's Blow** shows you everything you need to see in as little time as possible, then takes you to the best bars, nightclubs, and restaurants—where you'll really have fun—that most guidebooks skip. You'll laugh your way through Europe! *"Absolutely hilarious."* — Booklist. **$10.95**

Australia: Where the Fun Is by Lauren Goodyear & Thalassa Skinner. The "land down under" is becoming tops in travel for the young adult, and these recent Yale graduates spent a year combing Australia for the fun stuff. From the best bars in Sydney to the best beaches in New South Wales, this book will show you where and how to have a blast! *Available late 1990.* **$12.95**

––––––––

Mustang books should be available at your local bookstore. If not, send a check or money order for the price of the book — plus $1.50 for postage *per book* — to Mustang Publishing, P.O. Box 3004, Memphis, TN 38173. Allow three weeks for delivery. *For one week delivery, add $3.50 per book. Tennessee residents must add 7.75% sales tax. Foreign orders: U.S. funds only, please, and add $5.00 postage per book for Air Mail.*

3179